Turn the Page:

Unlocking the Story Within You

Coloring Book

Turn the Page:
Unlocking the Story Within You

Coloring Book

Dr. Johnny Parker

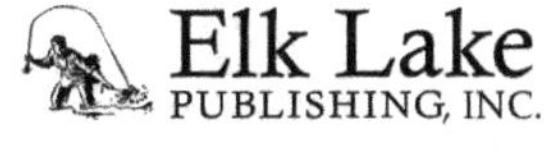

Elk Lake
PUBLISHING, INC.

Plymouth, Massachusetts

Cover Design and Illustrator: Ben Walker
Interior Design: Melinda Martin
Editor: Deb Haggerty
Published in Association with the Les Stobbe Agency

PUBLISHED BY: Elk Lake Publishing, Inc., 35 Dogwood Dr., Plymouth, MA 02360

Library Cataloging Data
Names: Parker, Dr. Johnny C. (Dr. Johnny C. Parker)
Turn the Page Coloring Book/ Dr. Johnny C. Parker
58 p. 20 cm × 25cm (8 in × 10 in.)
Description: Elk Lake Publishing, Inc. POD | Elk Lake Publishing, Inc. Trade paperback edition | Elk Lake Publishing, Inc. 2016.
Identifiers: ISBN-13: 978-1-946638-06-9 (POD) | 978-1-946638-04-05 (Trade)
Key Words: animals, adults, coloring, creative, art, relaxation, inspiration.
508746173404072017 NF

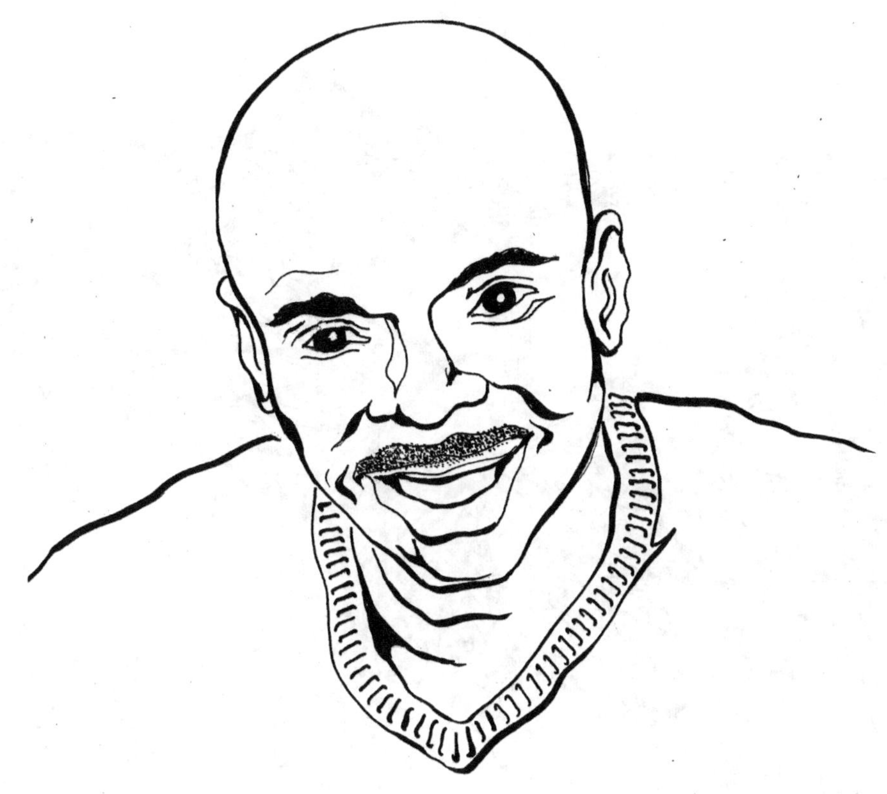

Coloring has many positive benefits and can support you in turning the page. Through coloring, you will be able to experience a calming mindset, strong clarity, and presence in the moment. So, pick up a colored pencil or crayon and color. Allow yourself to relax and begin to enrich your story.

—**Dr. Johnny Parker**,
Author of *Turn the Page: Unlocking the Story Within You*

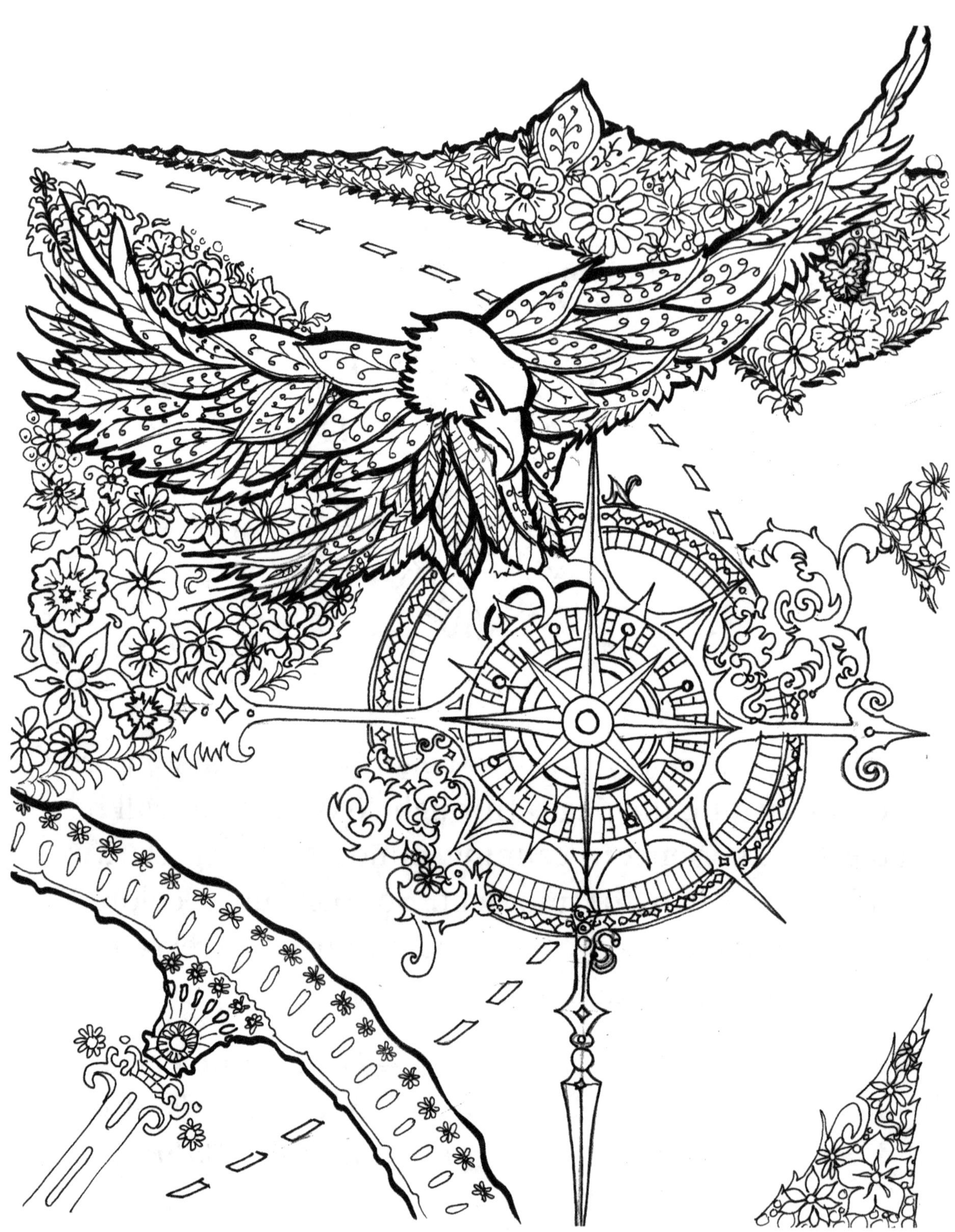

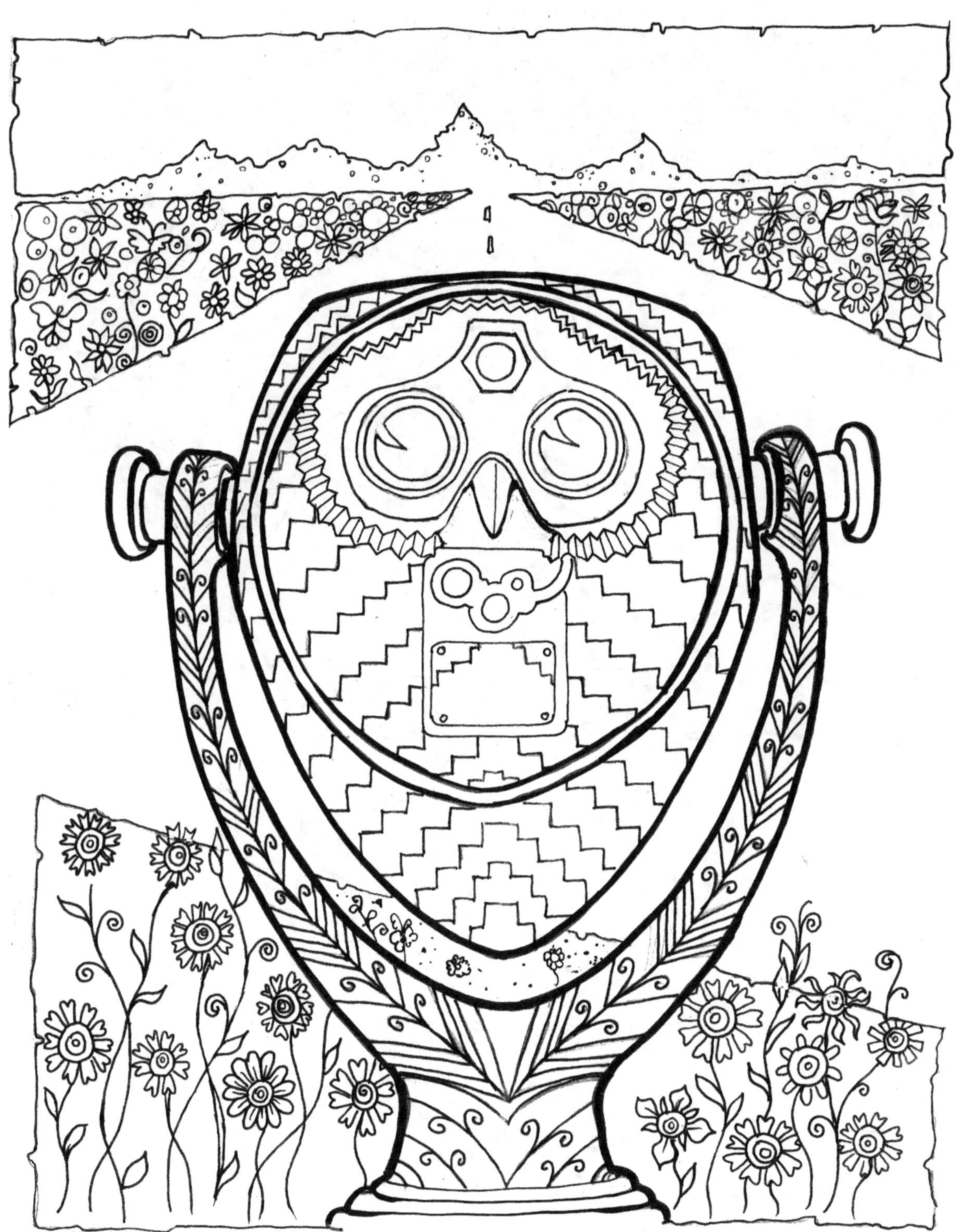

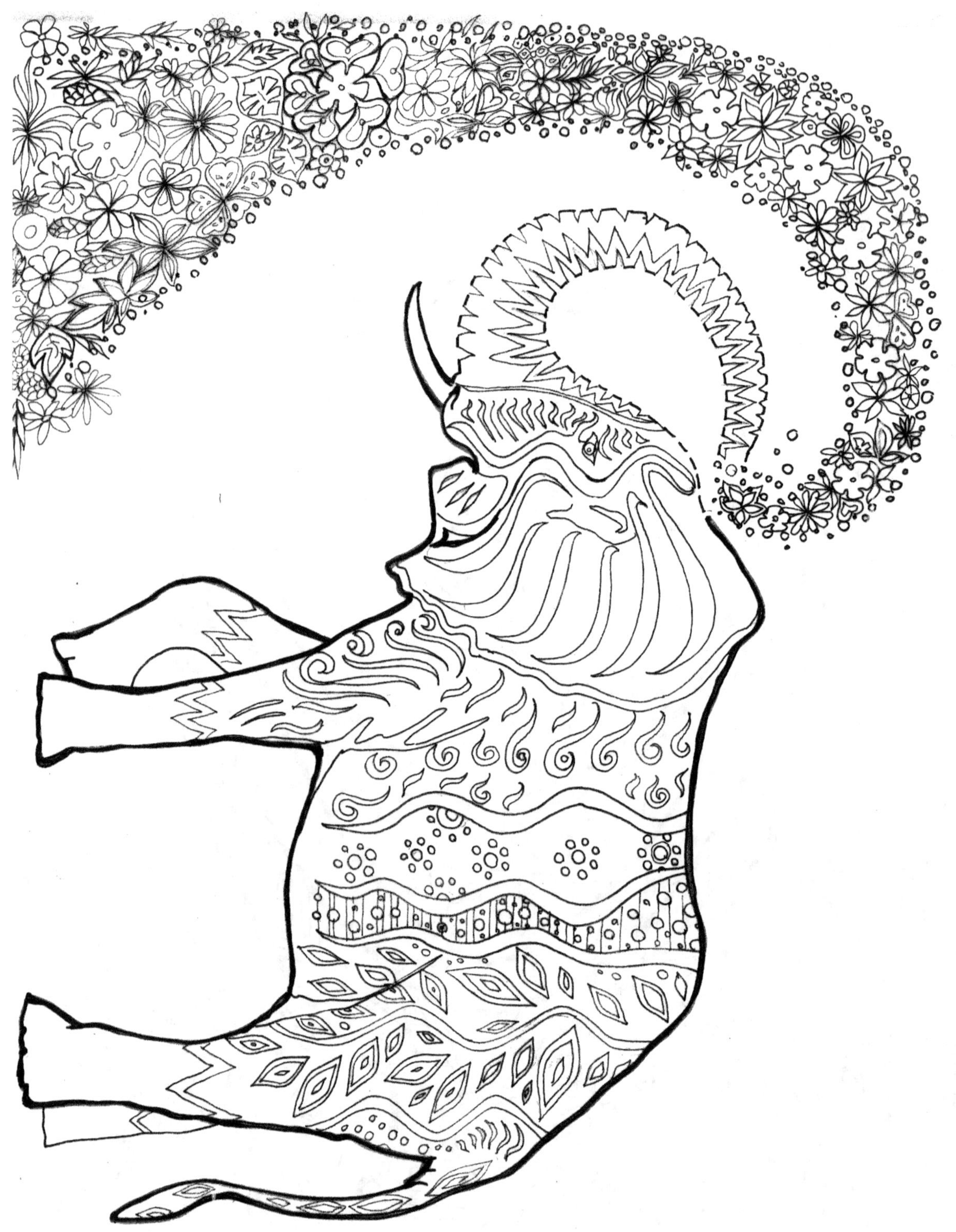

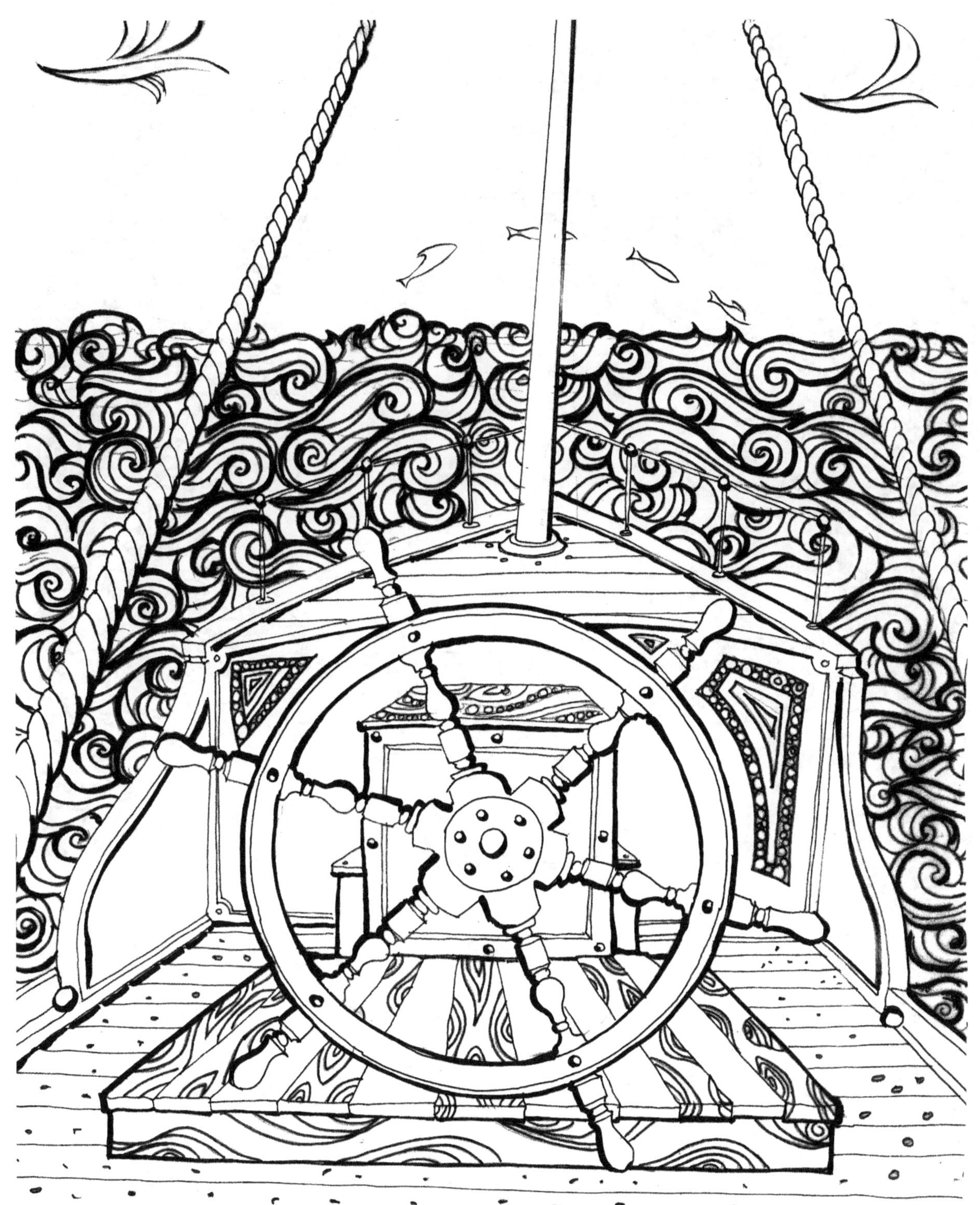

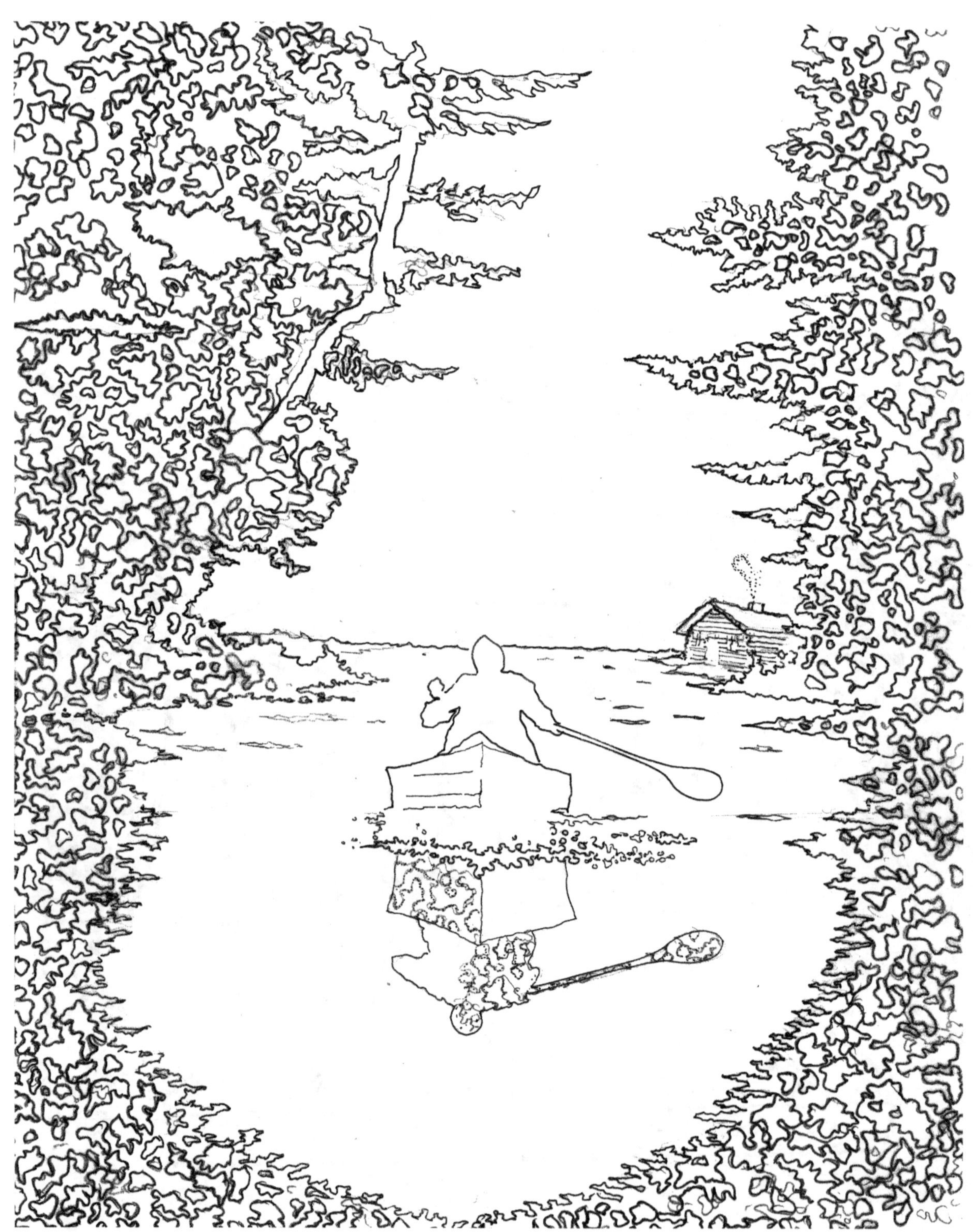

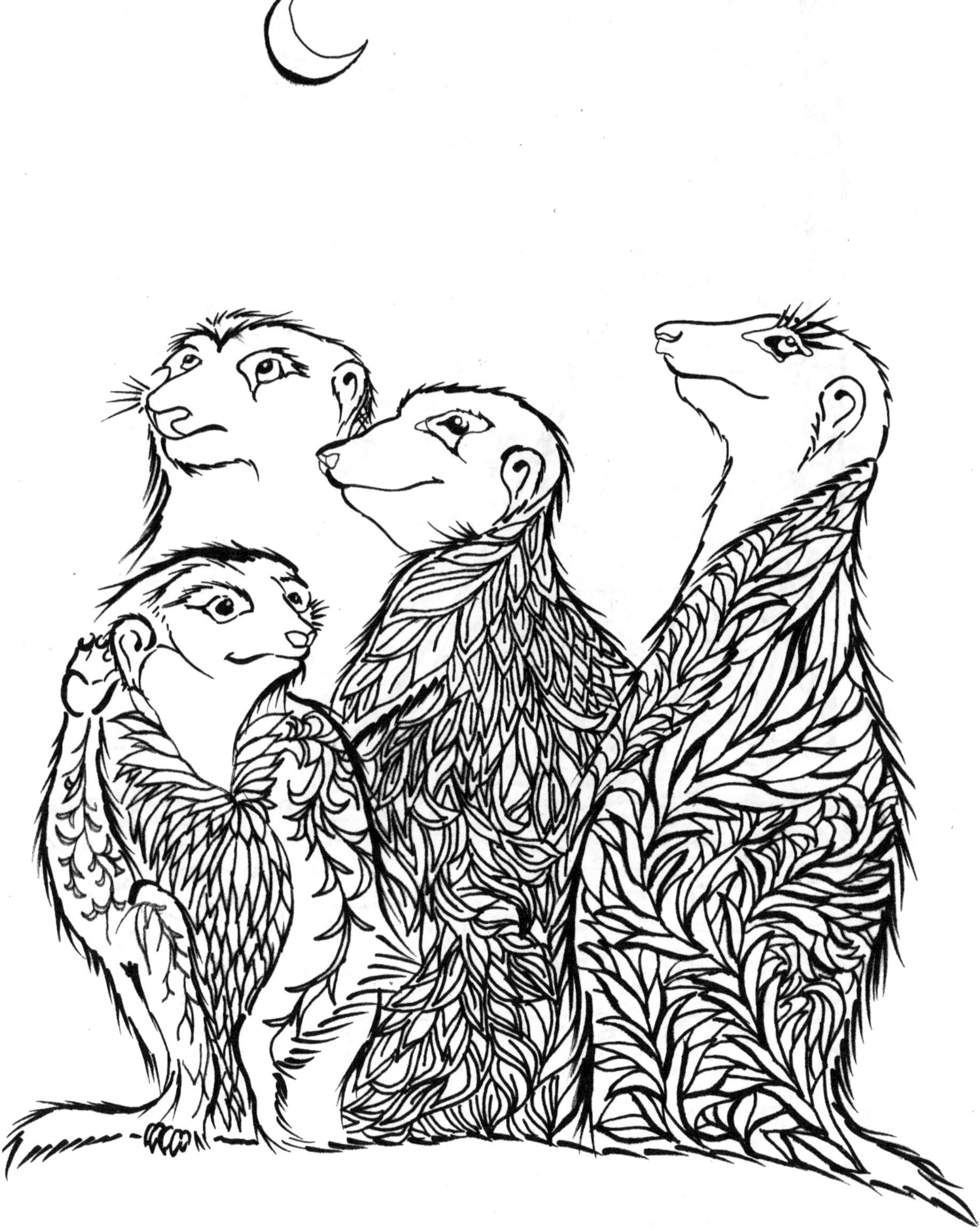

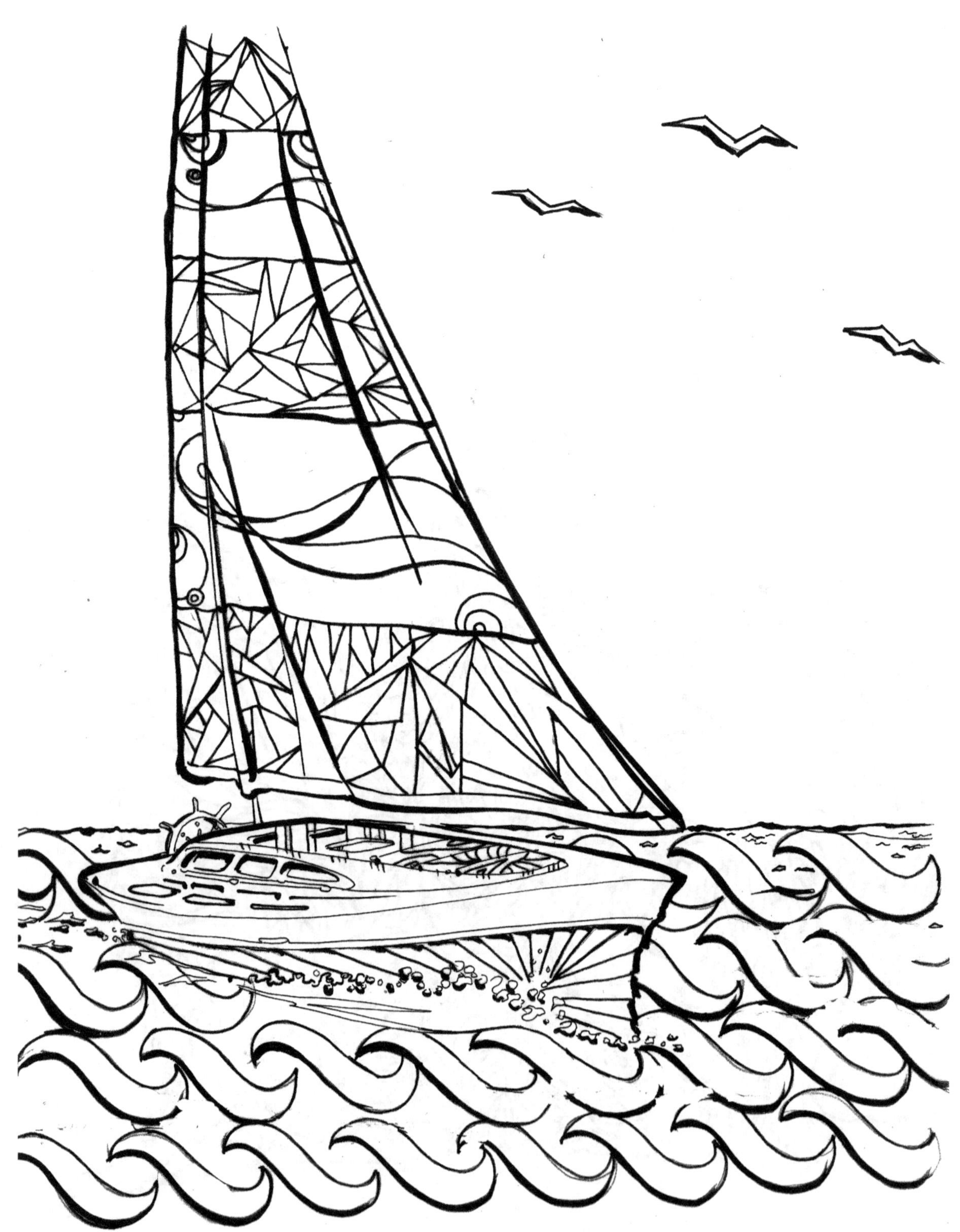

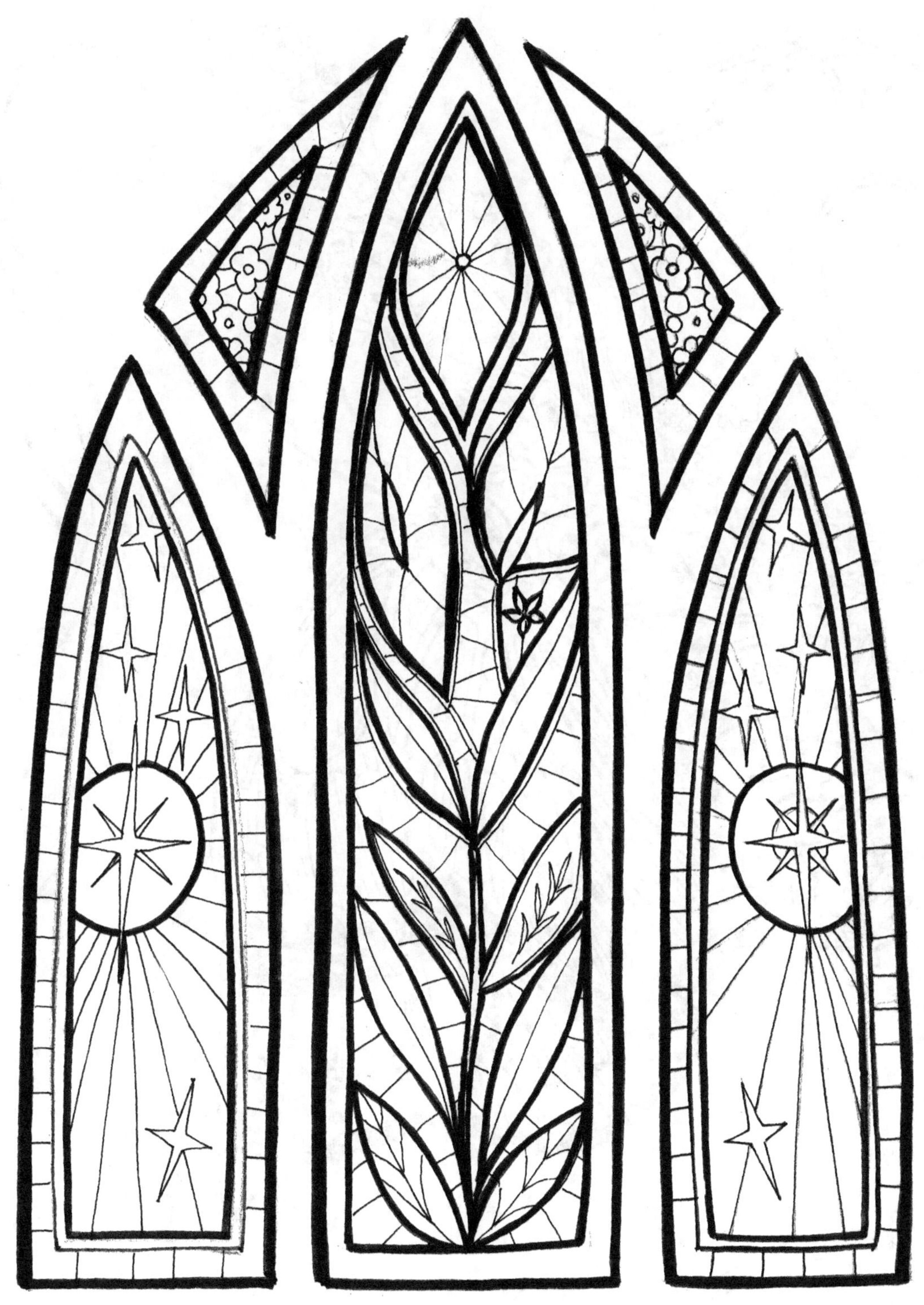

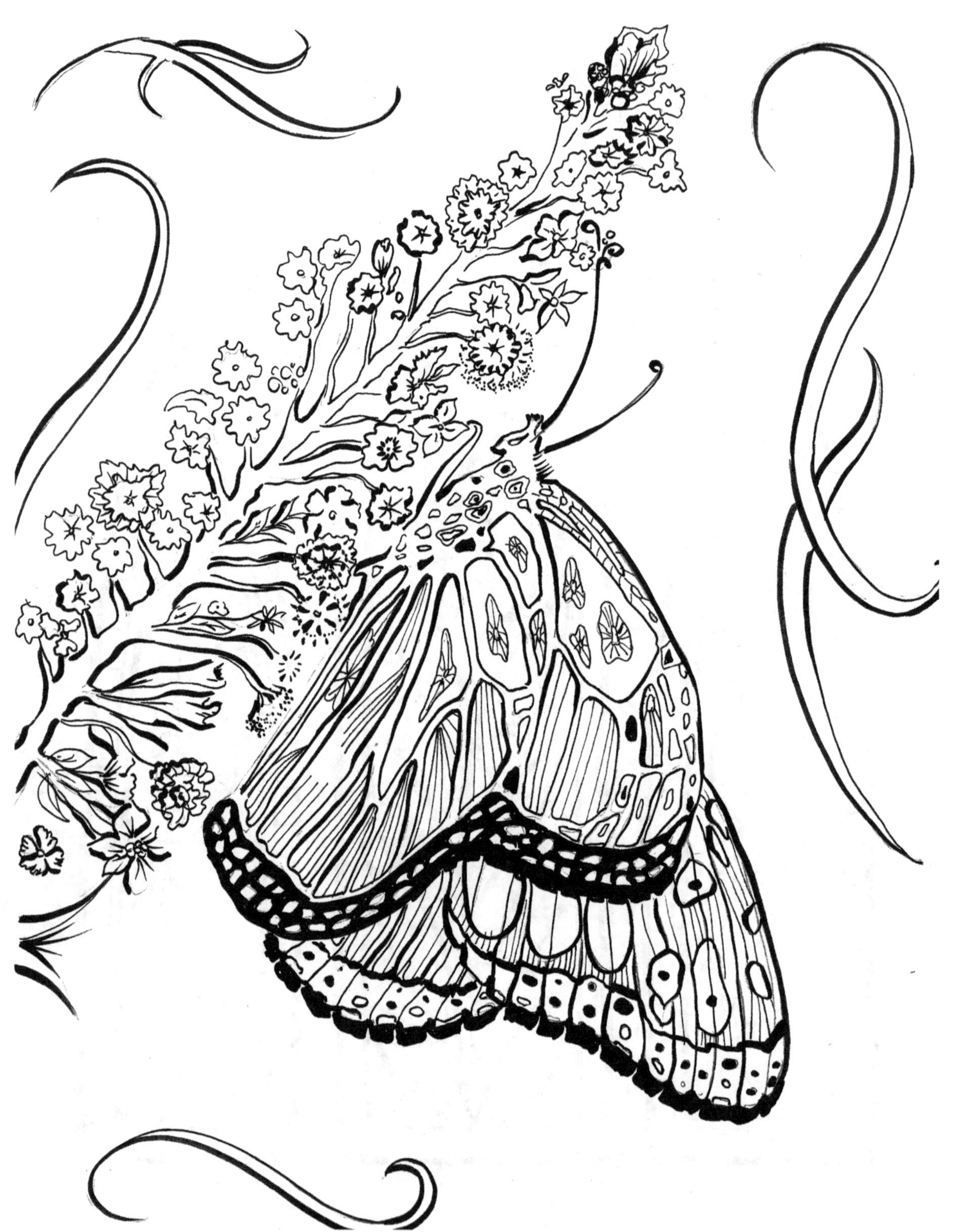

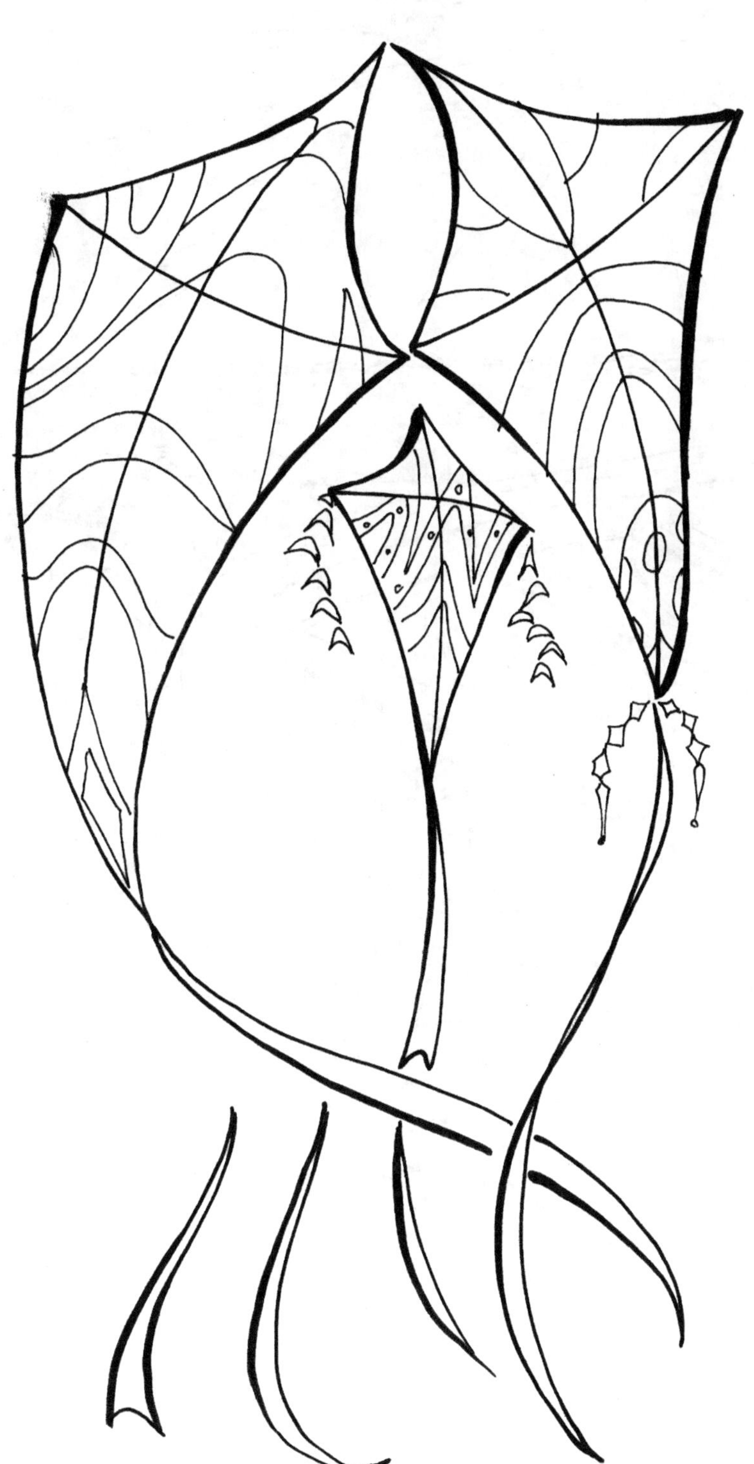

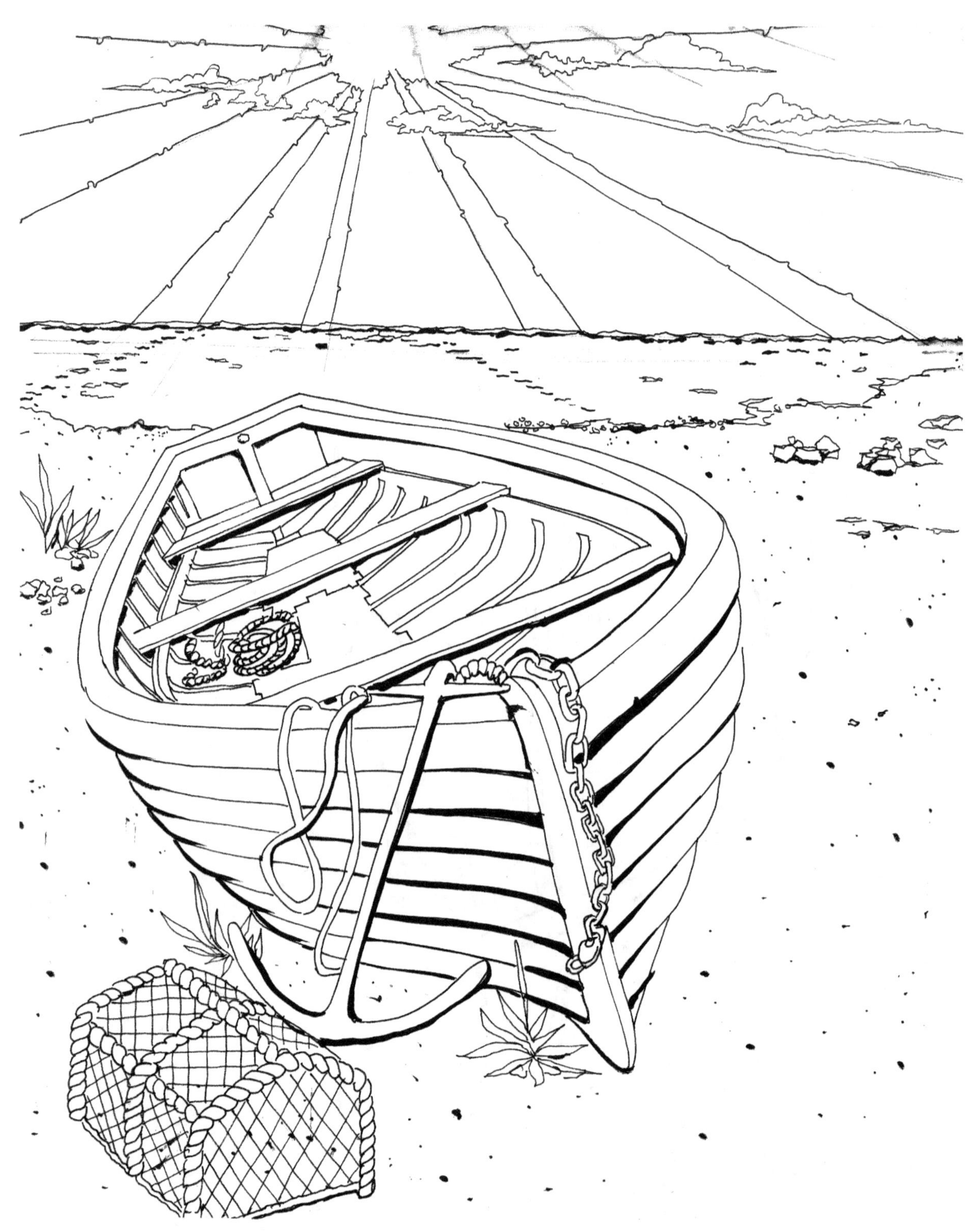

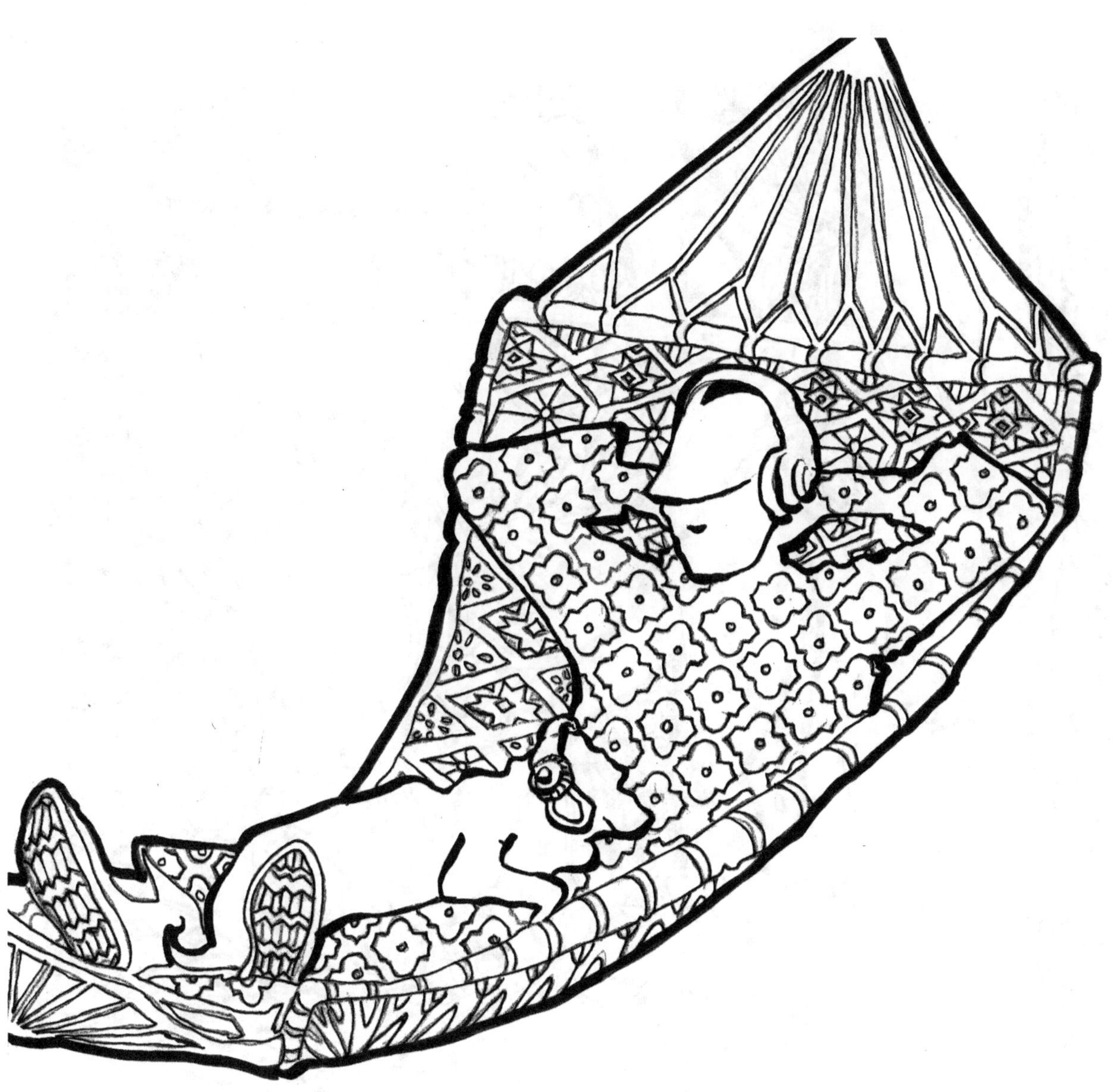

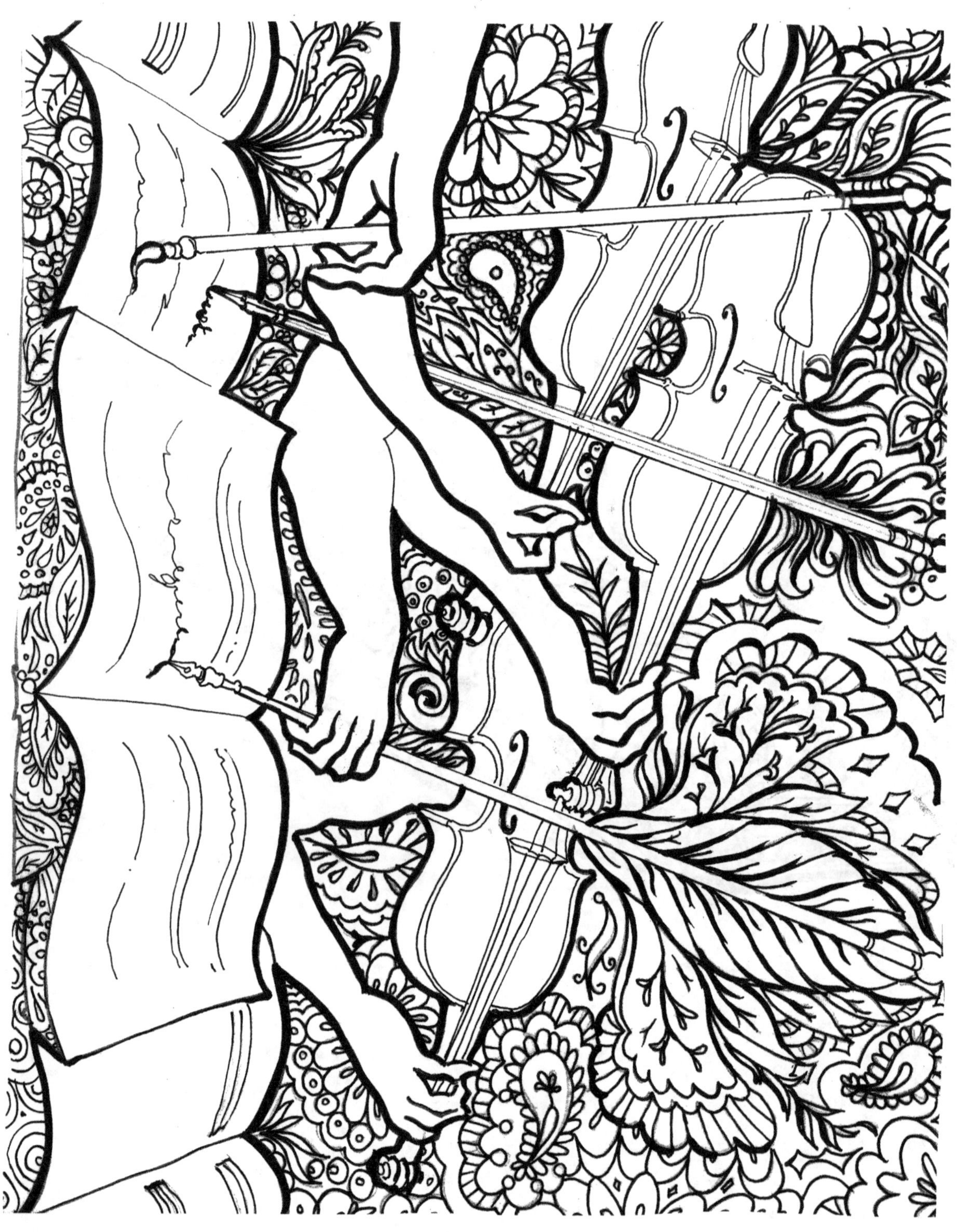

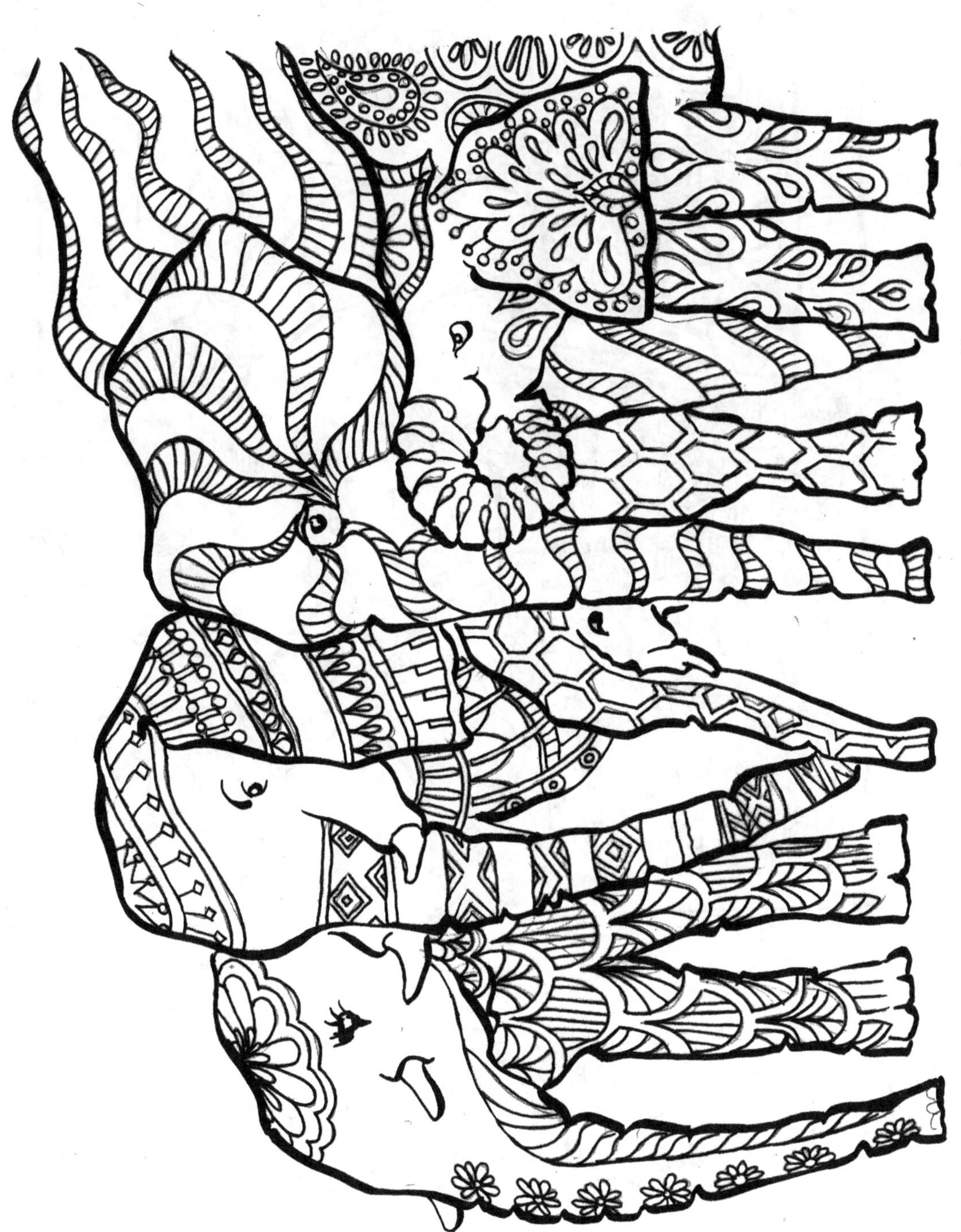

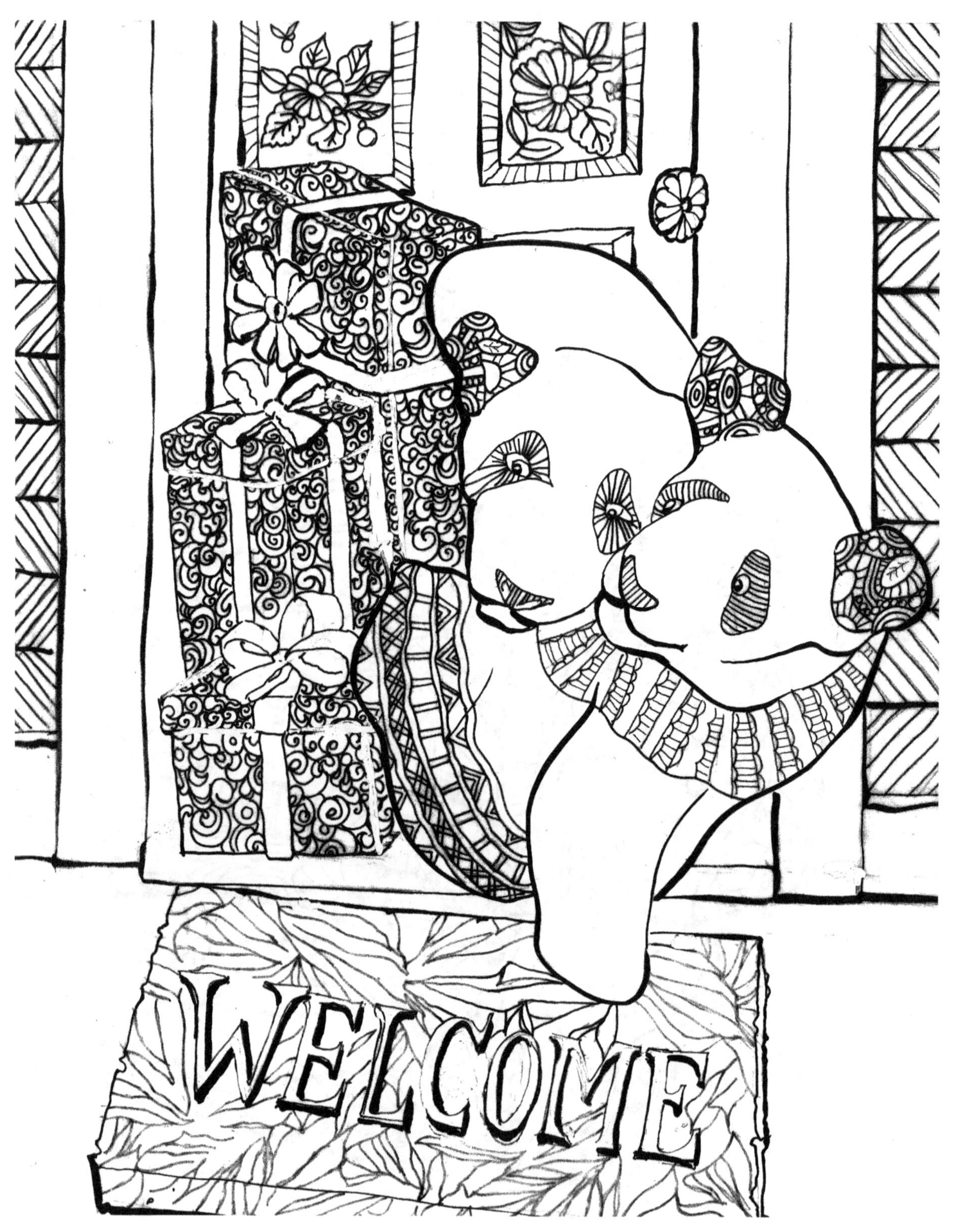
WELCOME

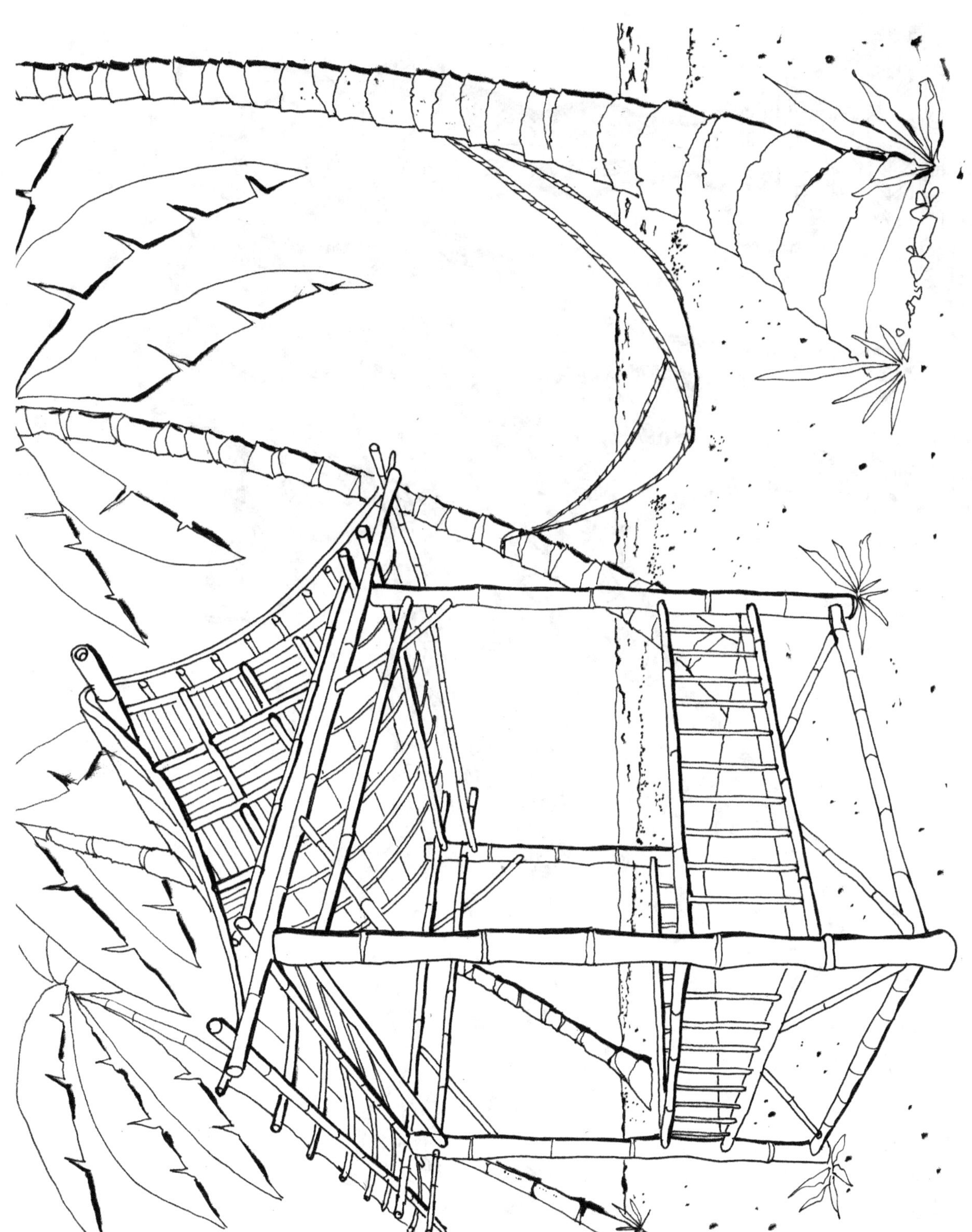

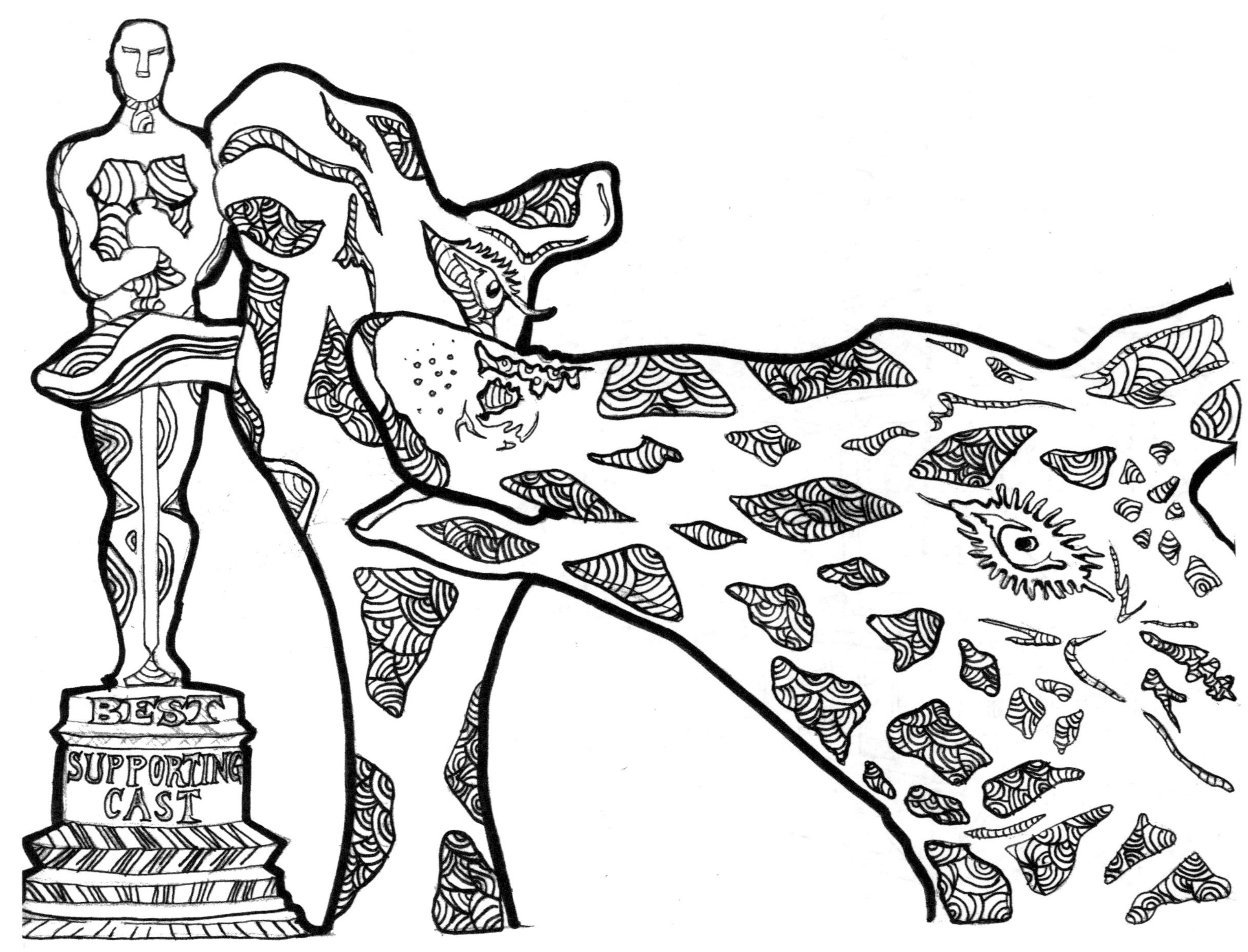
BEST
SUPPORTING
CAST

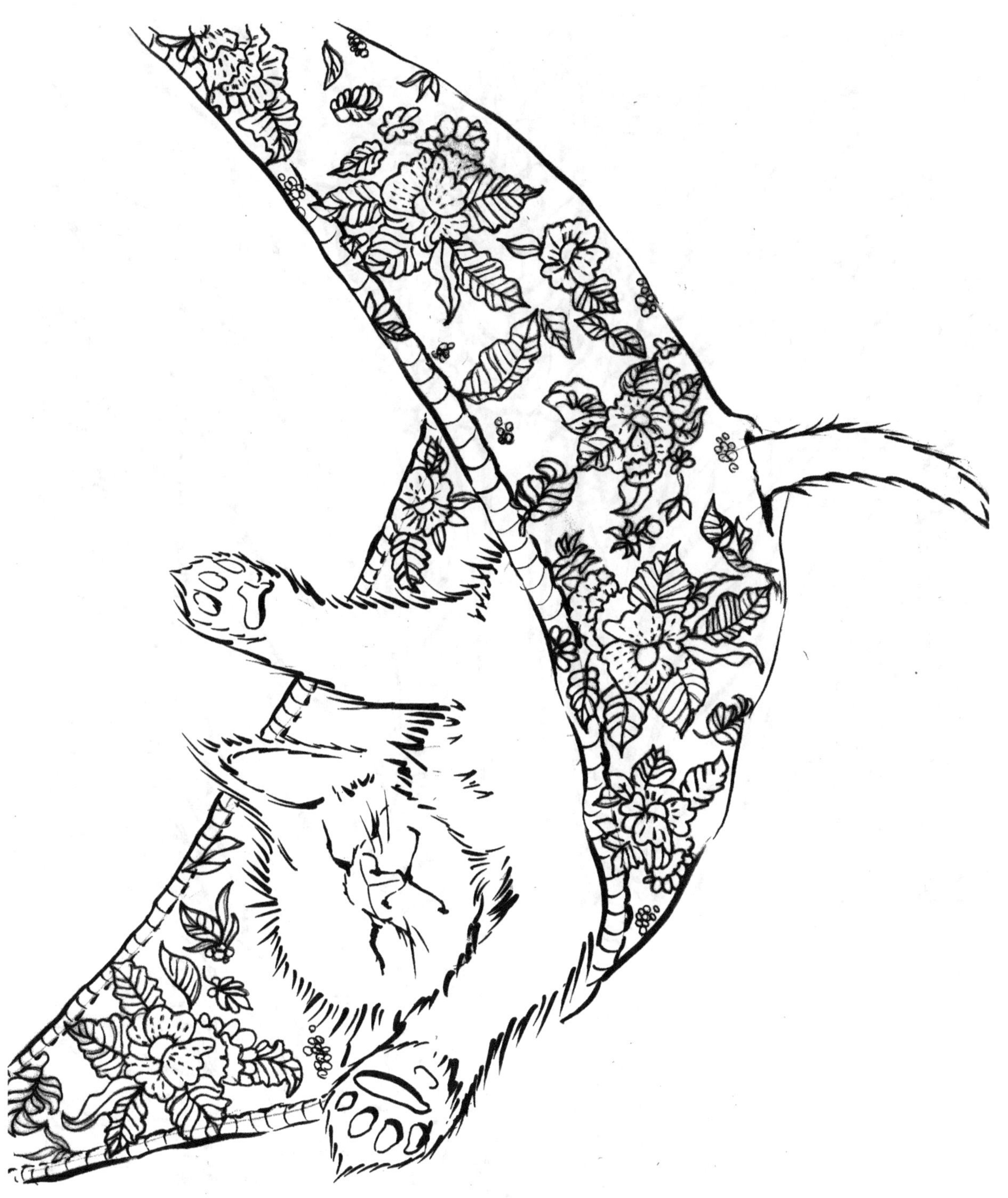

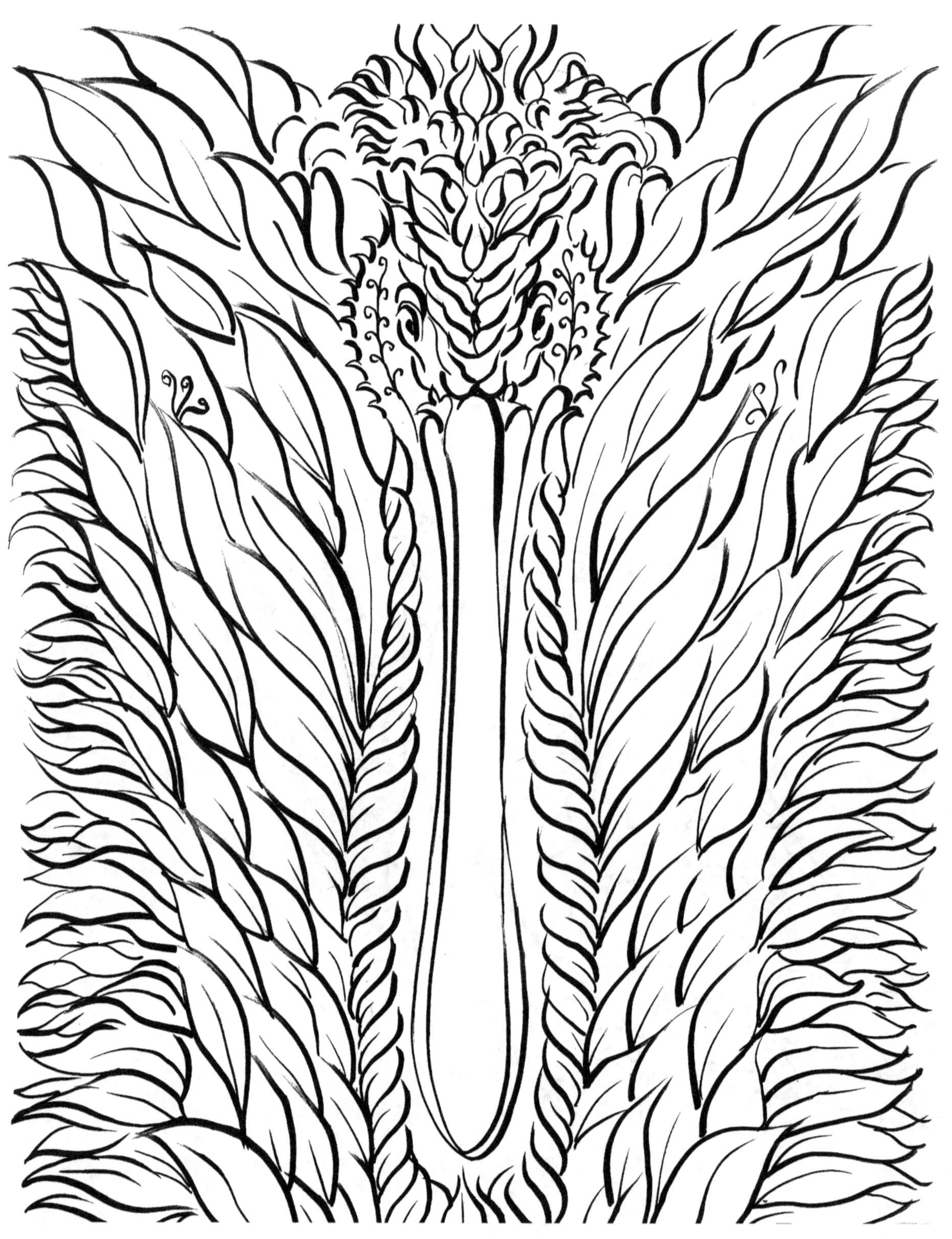

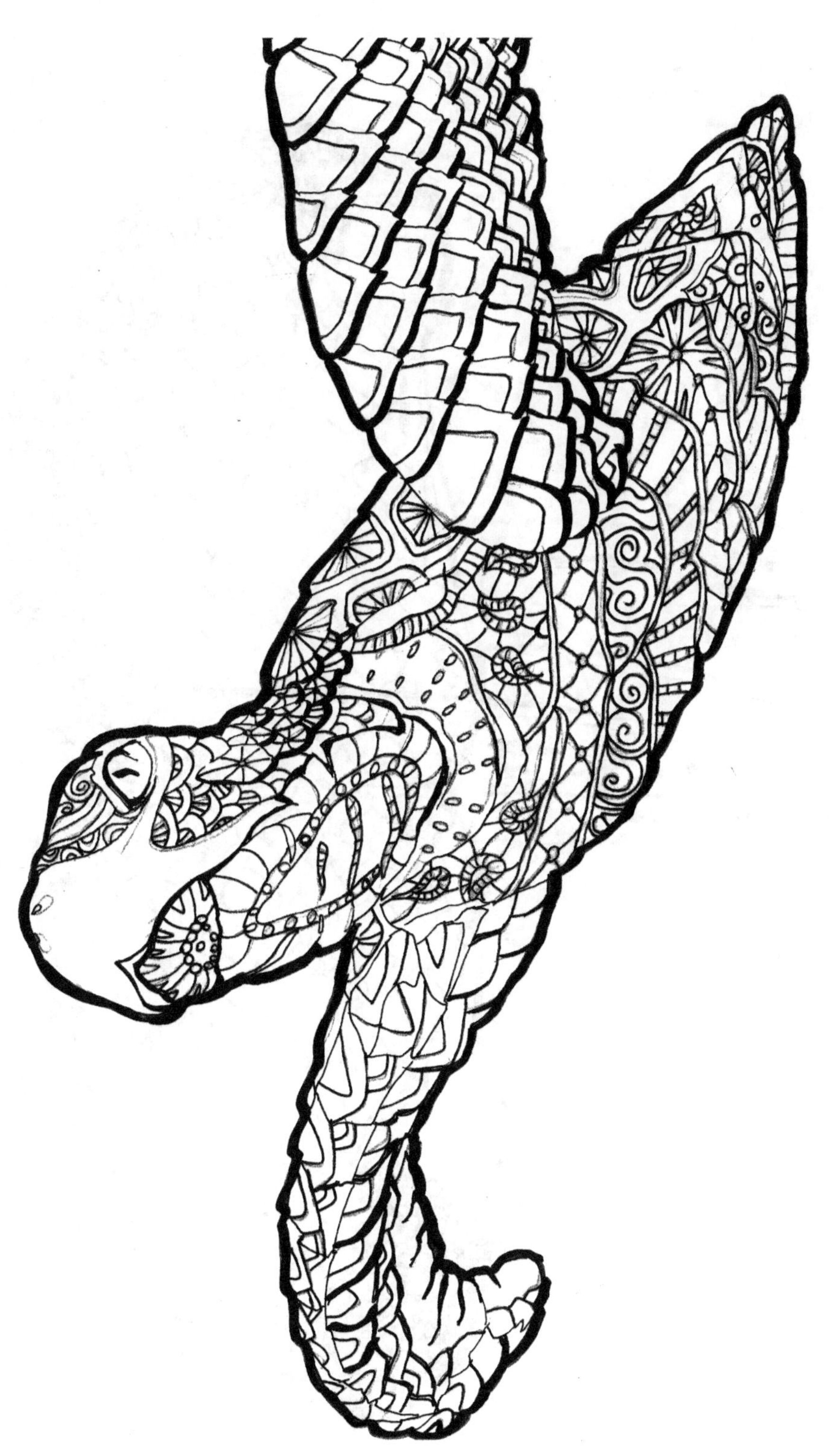

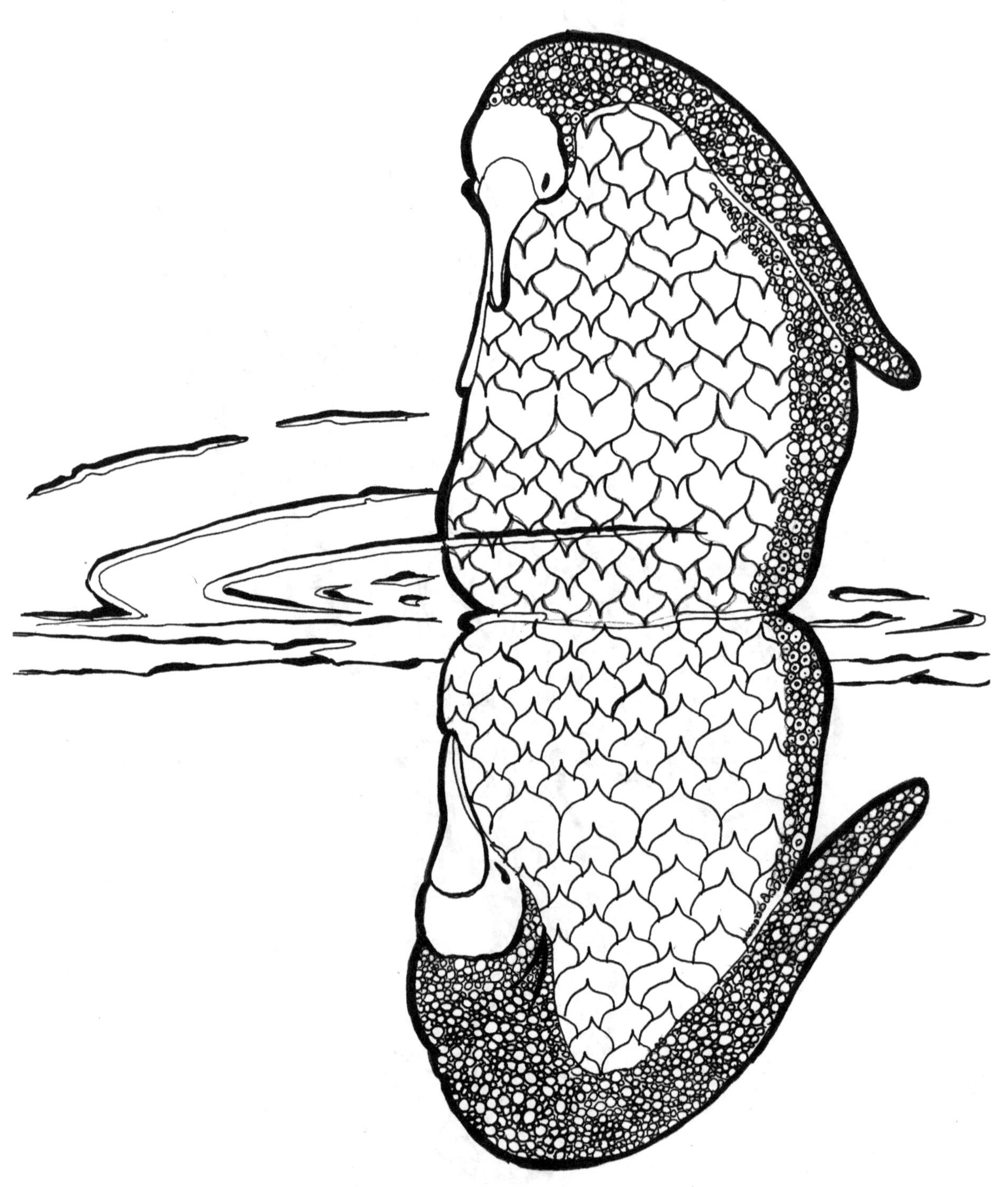

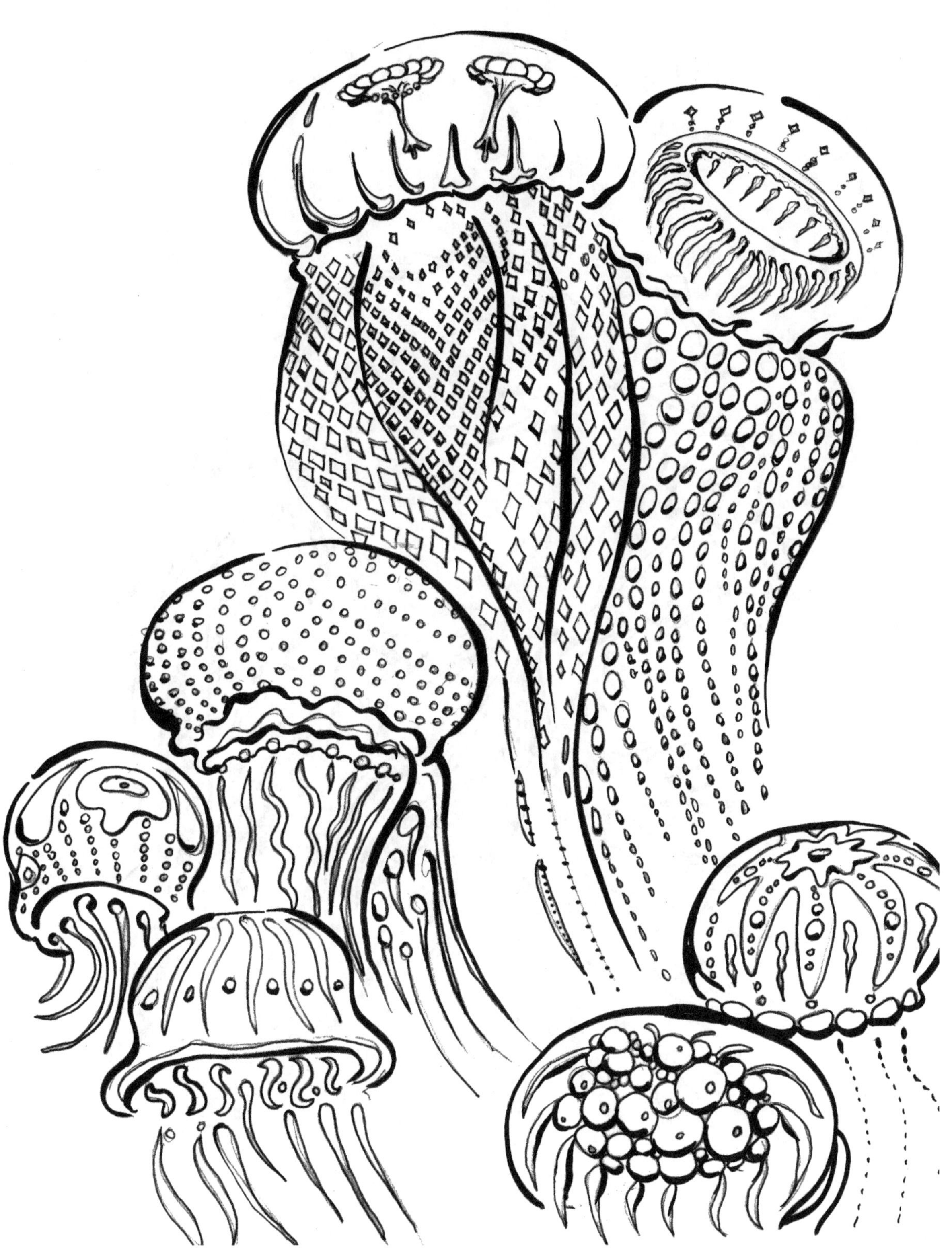

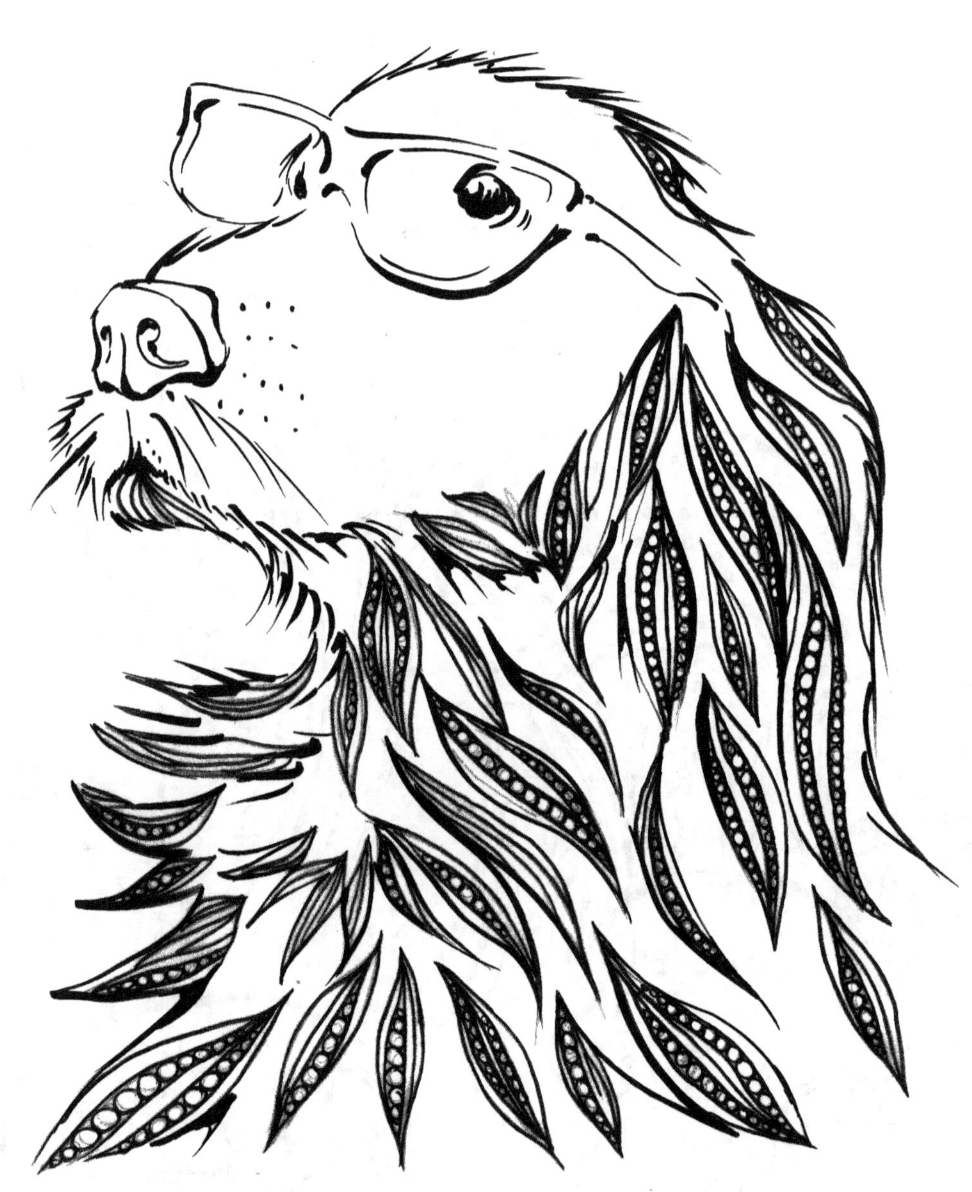

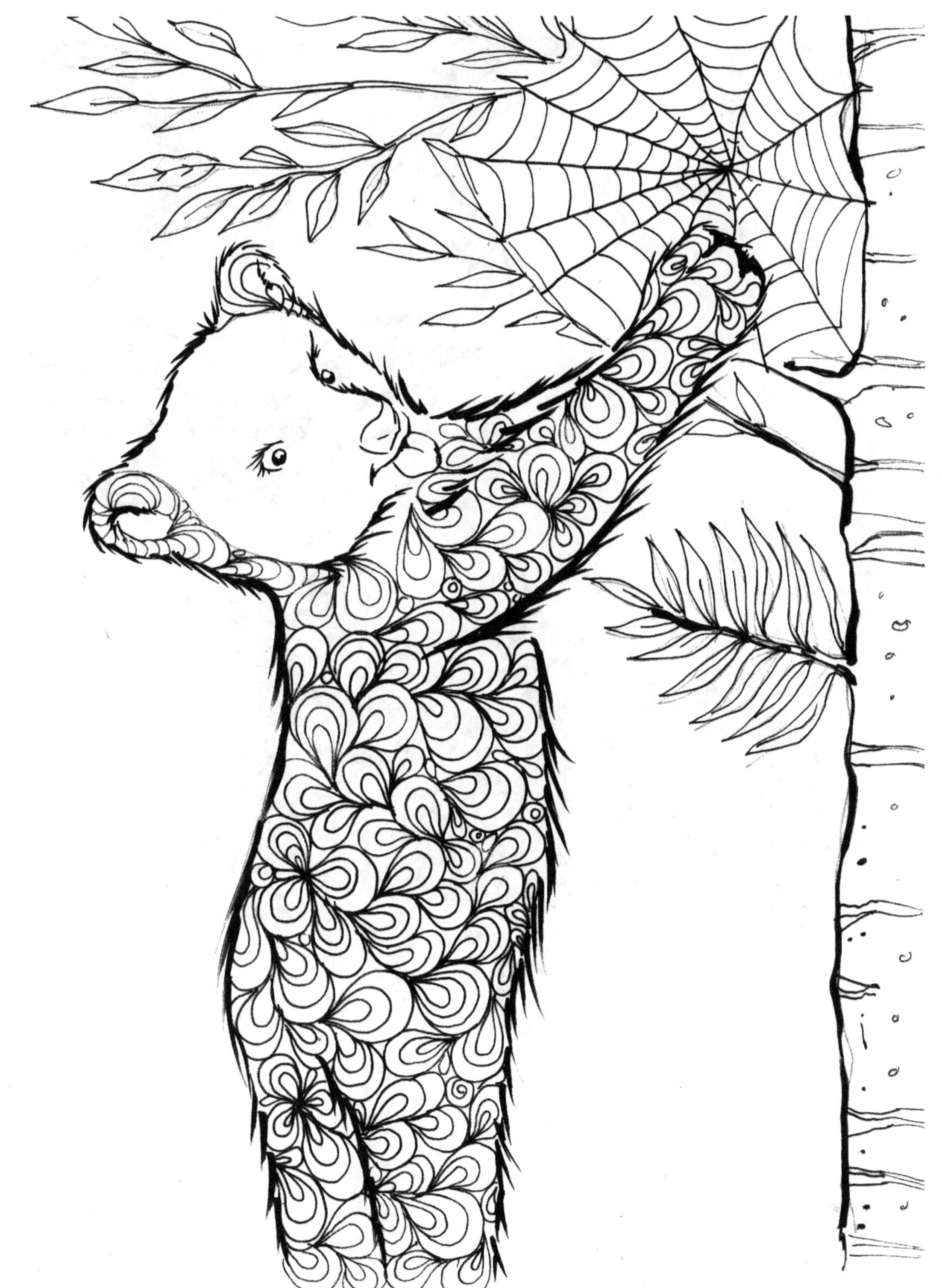

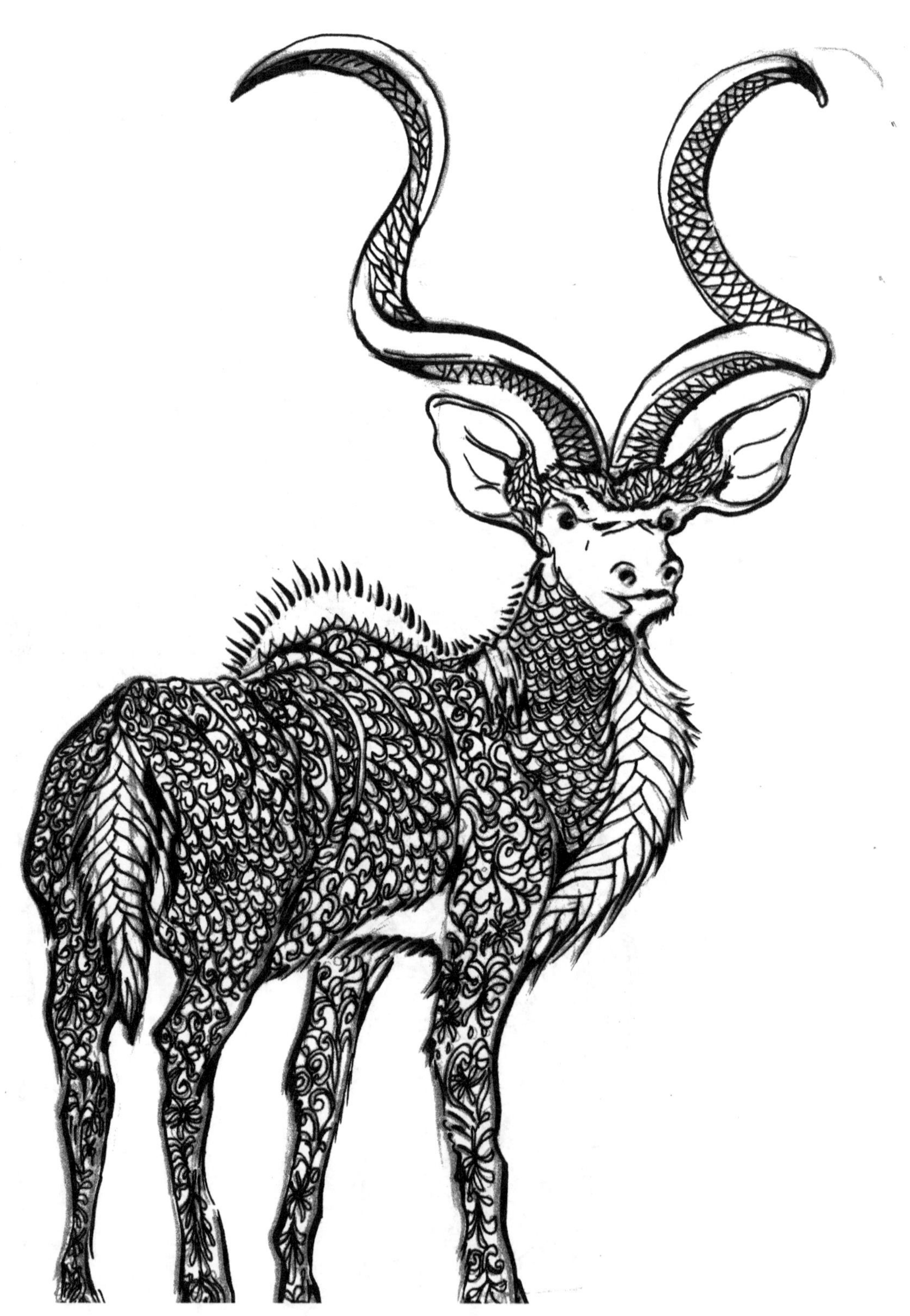

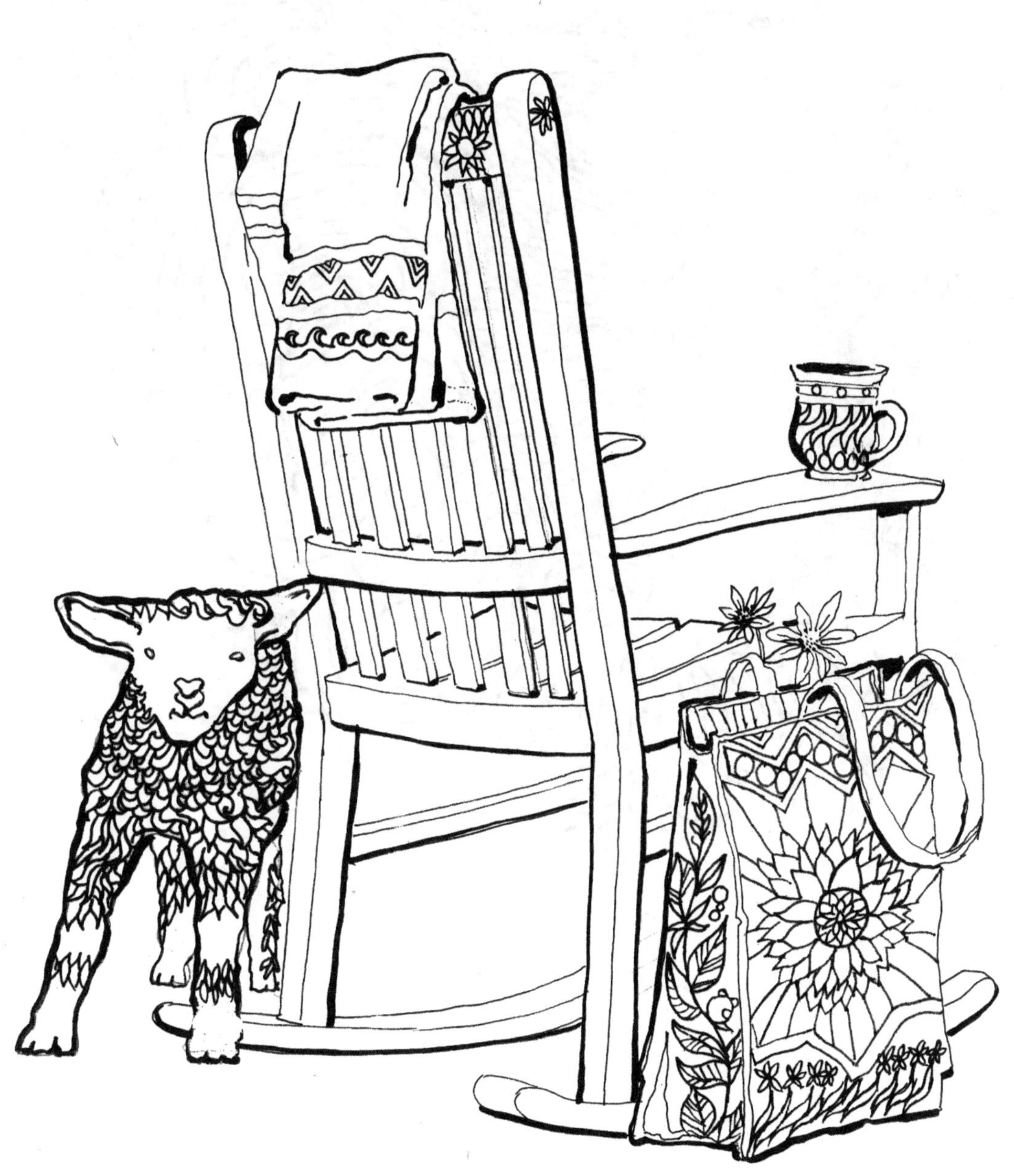

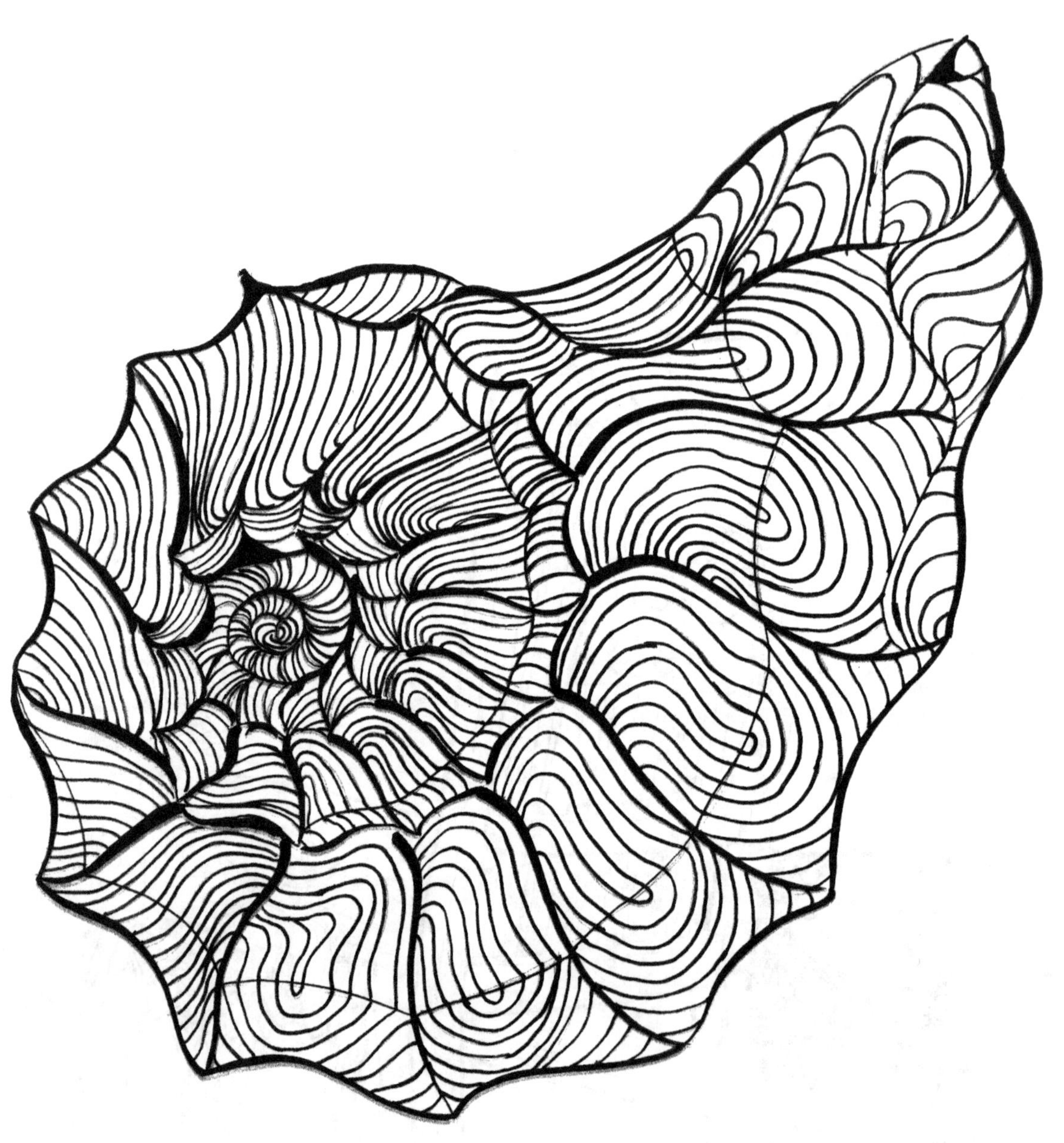

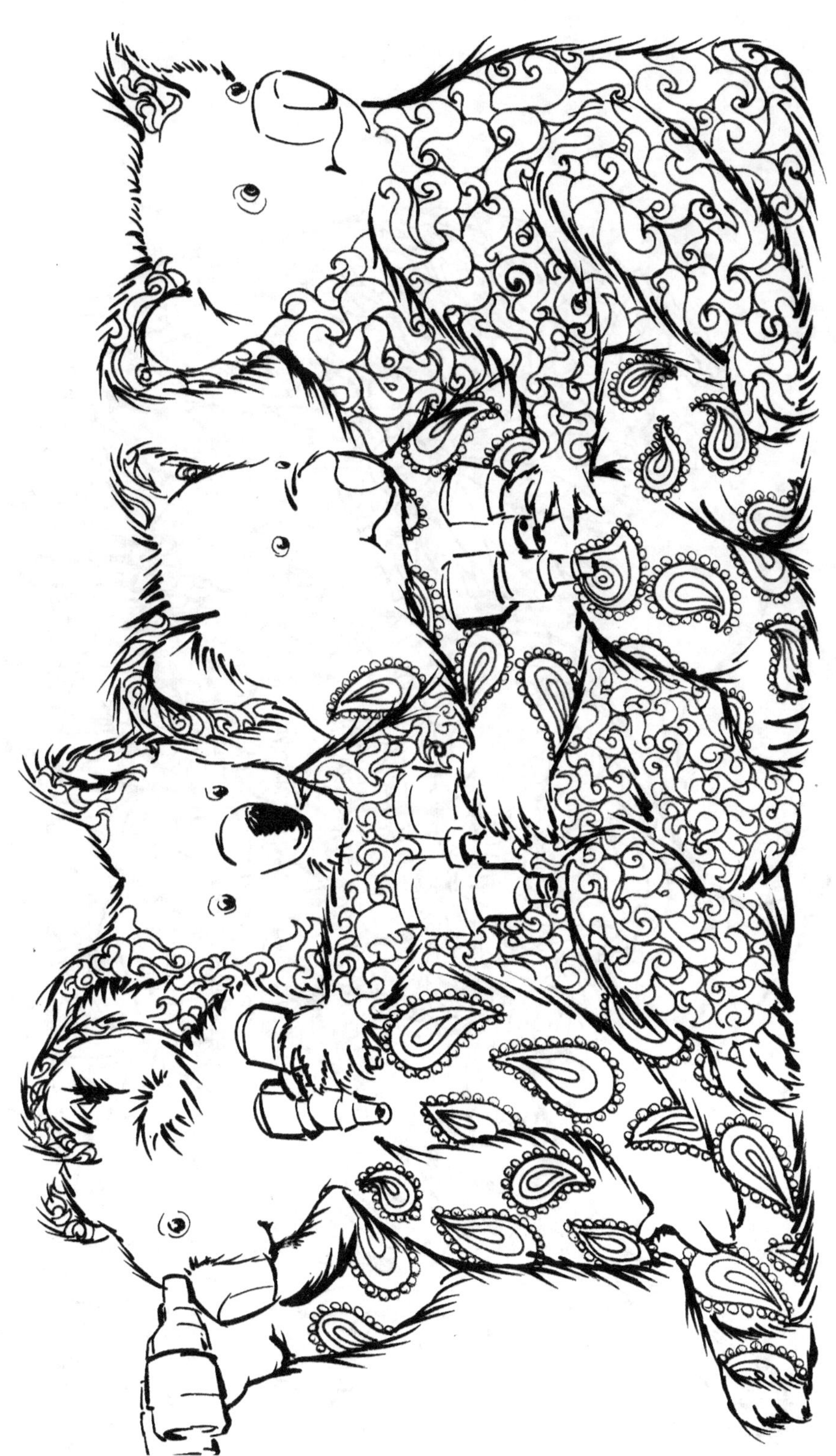

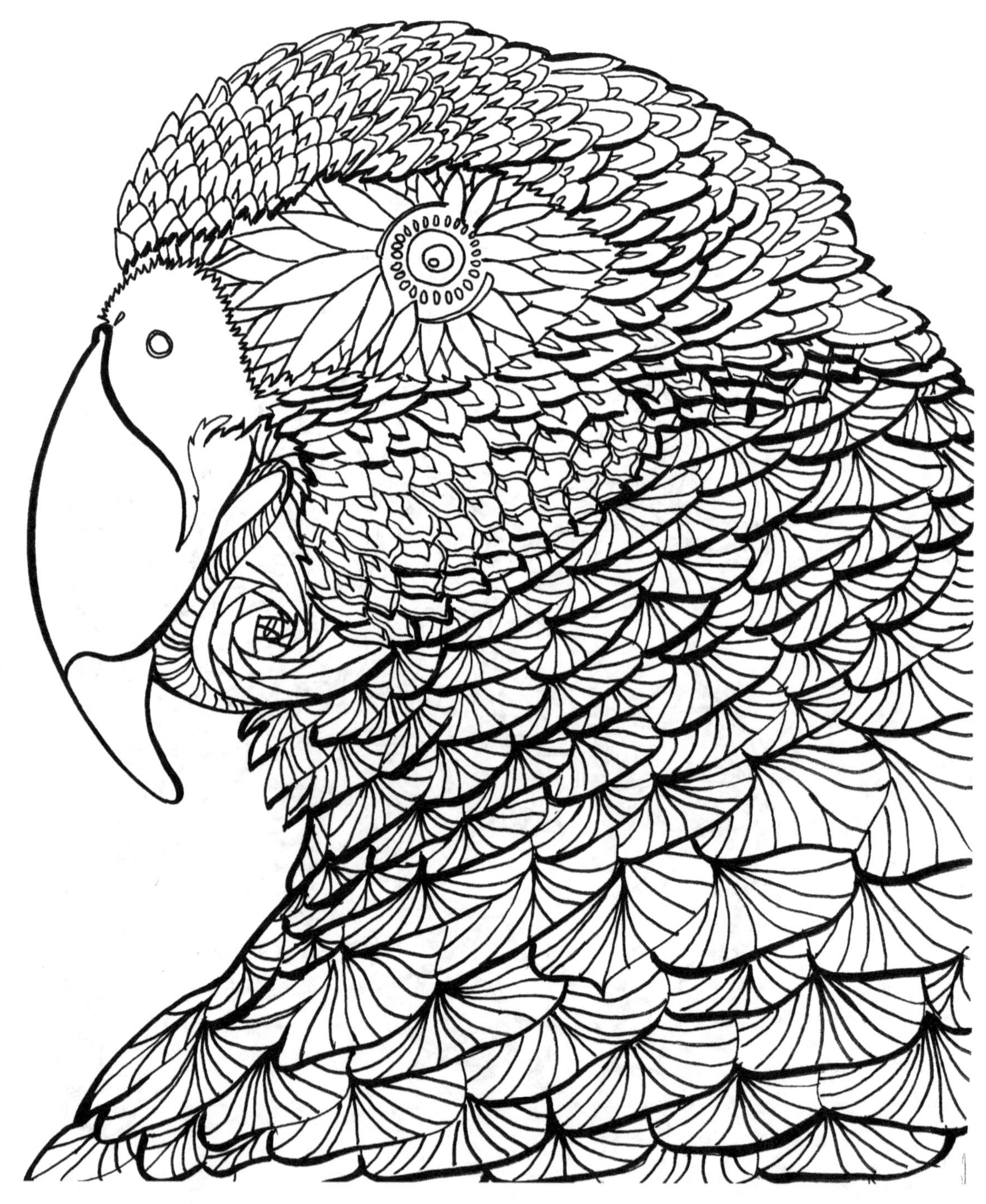

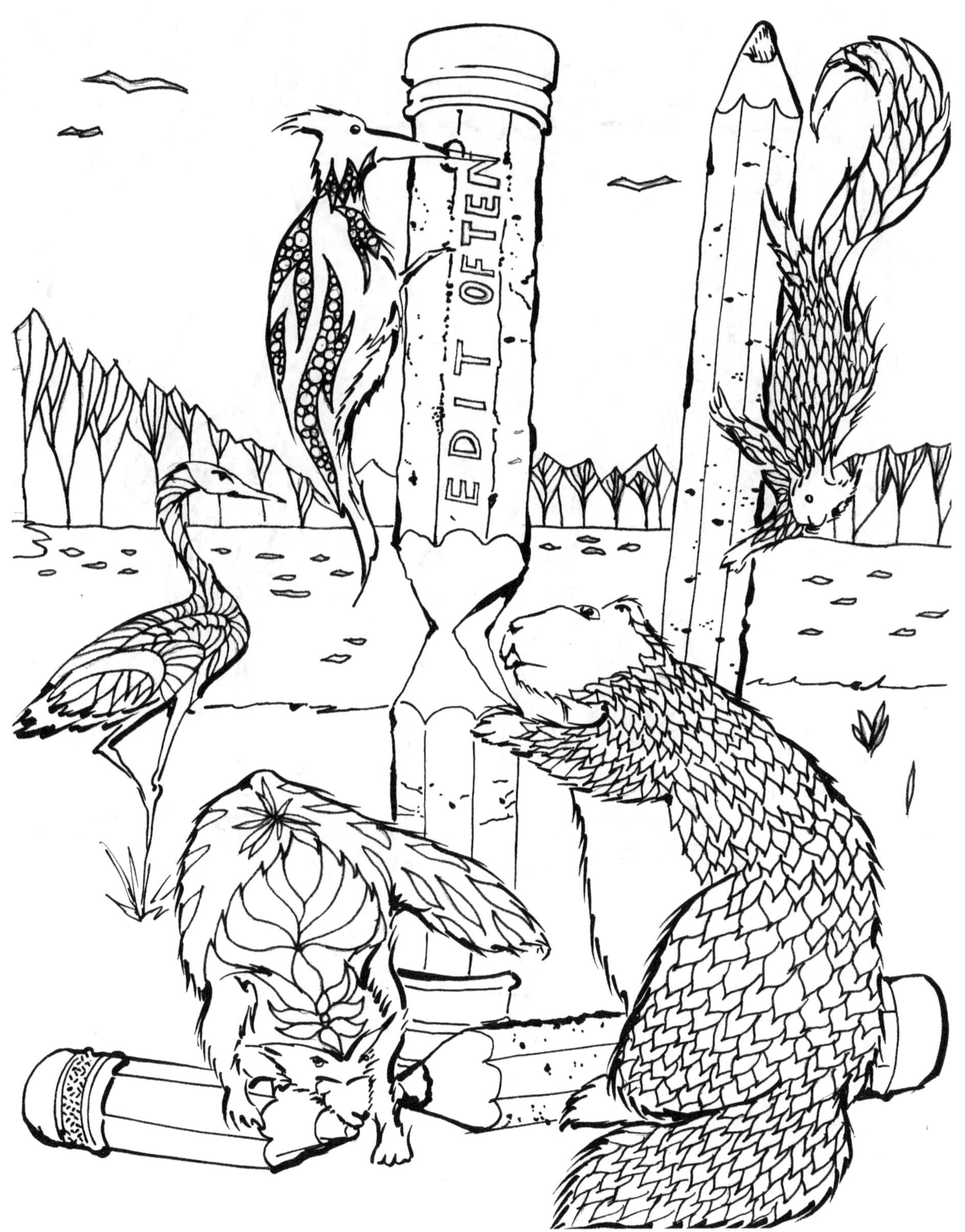
EDIT OFTEN

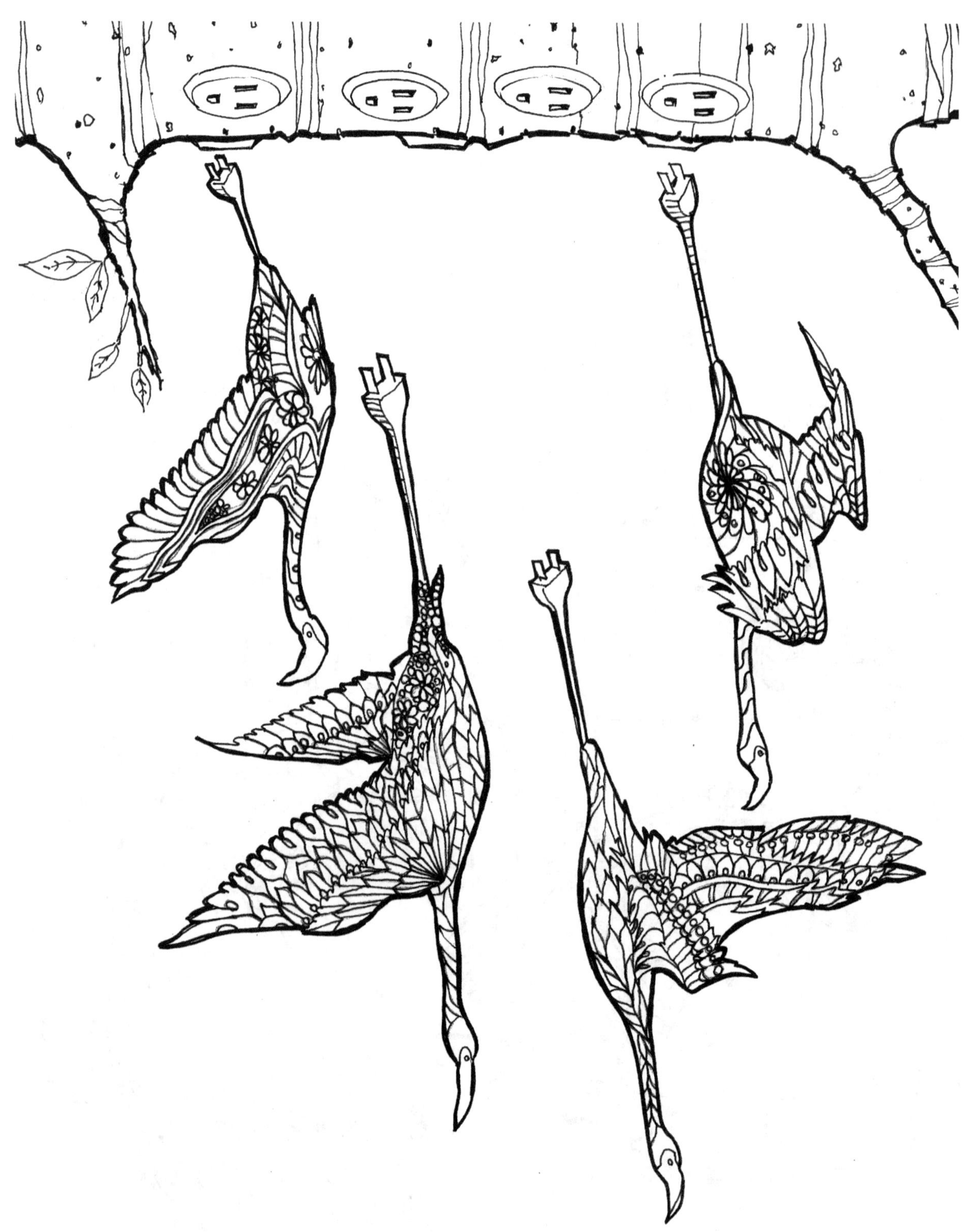

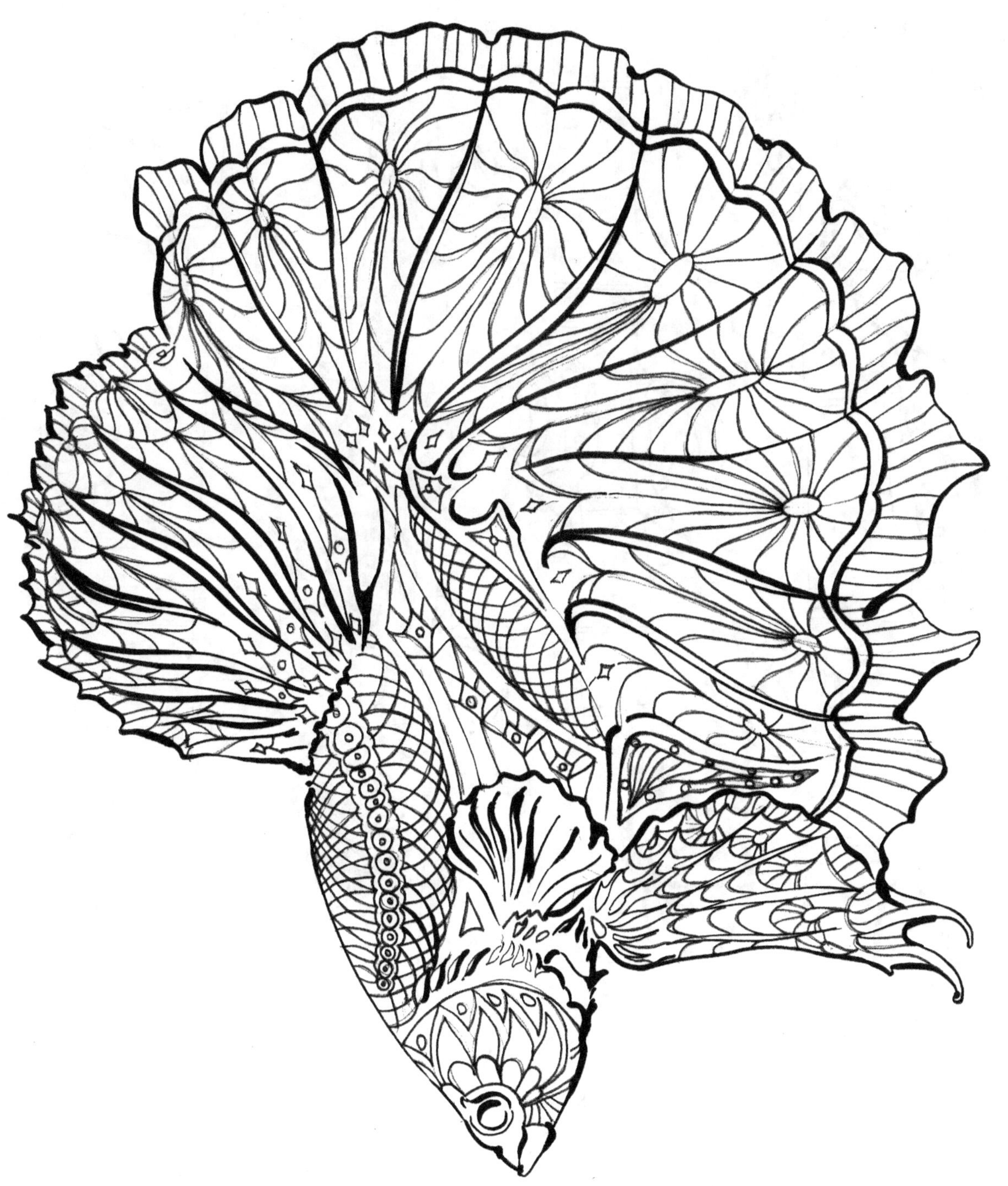

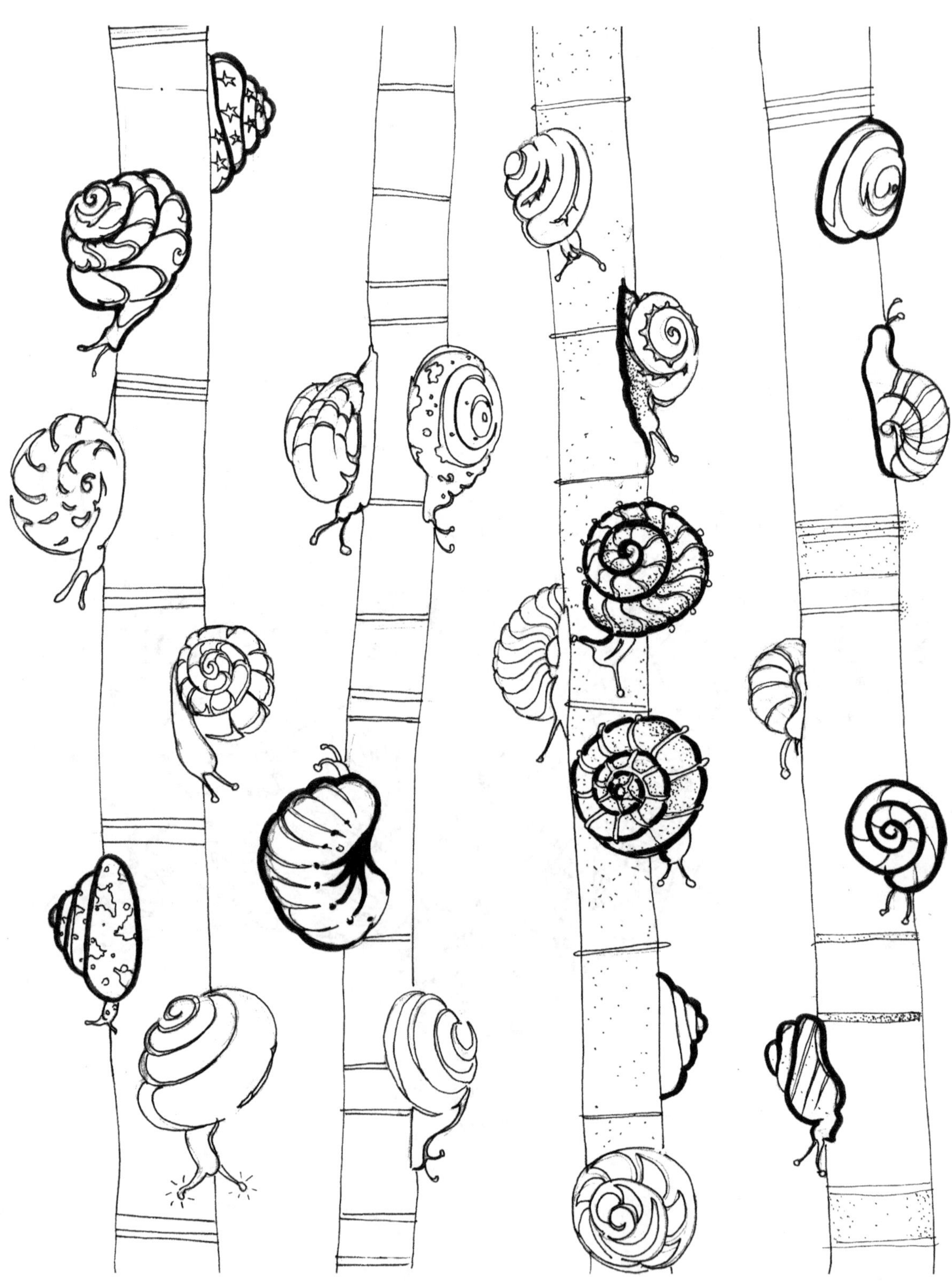

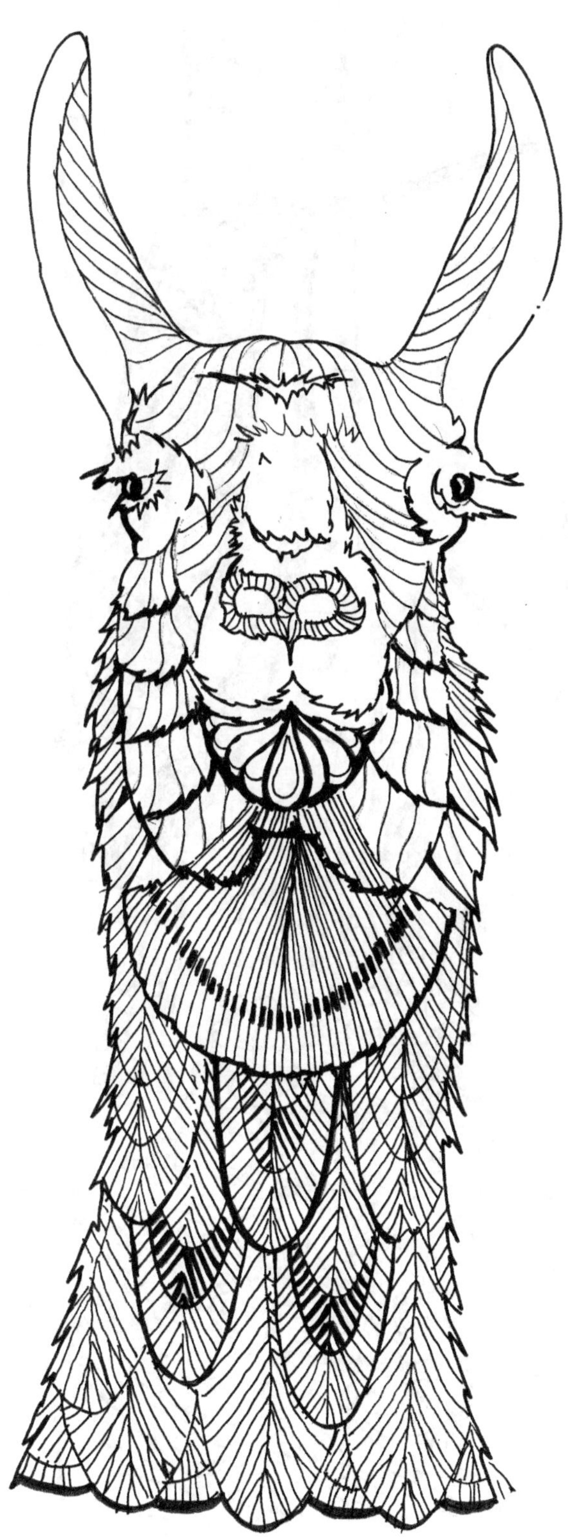

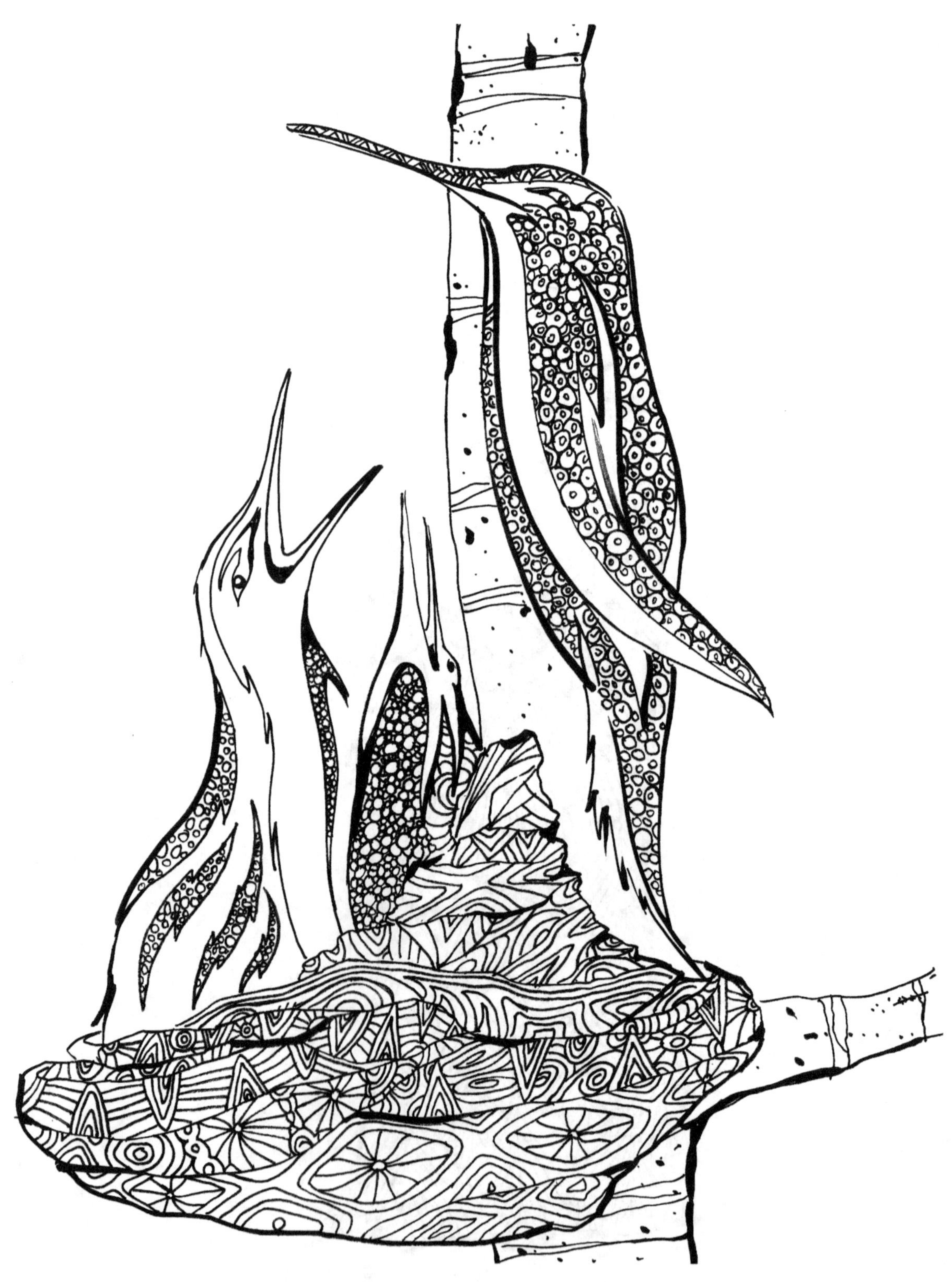

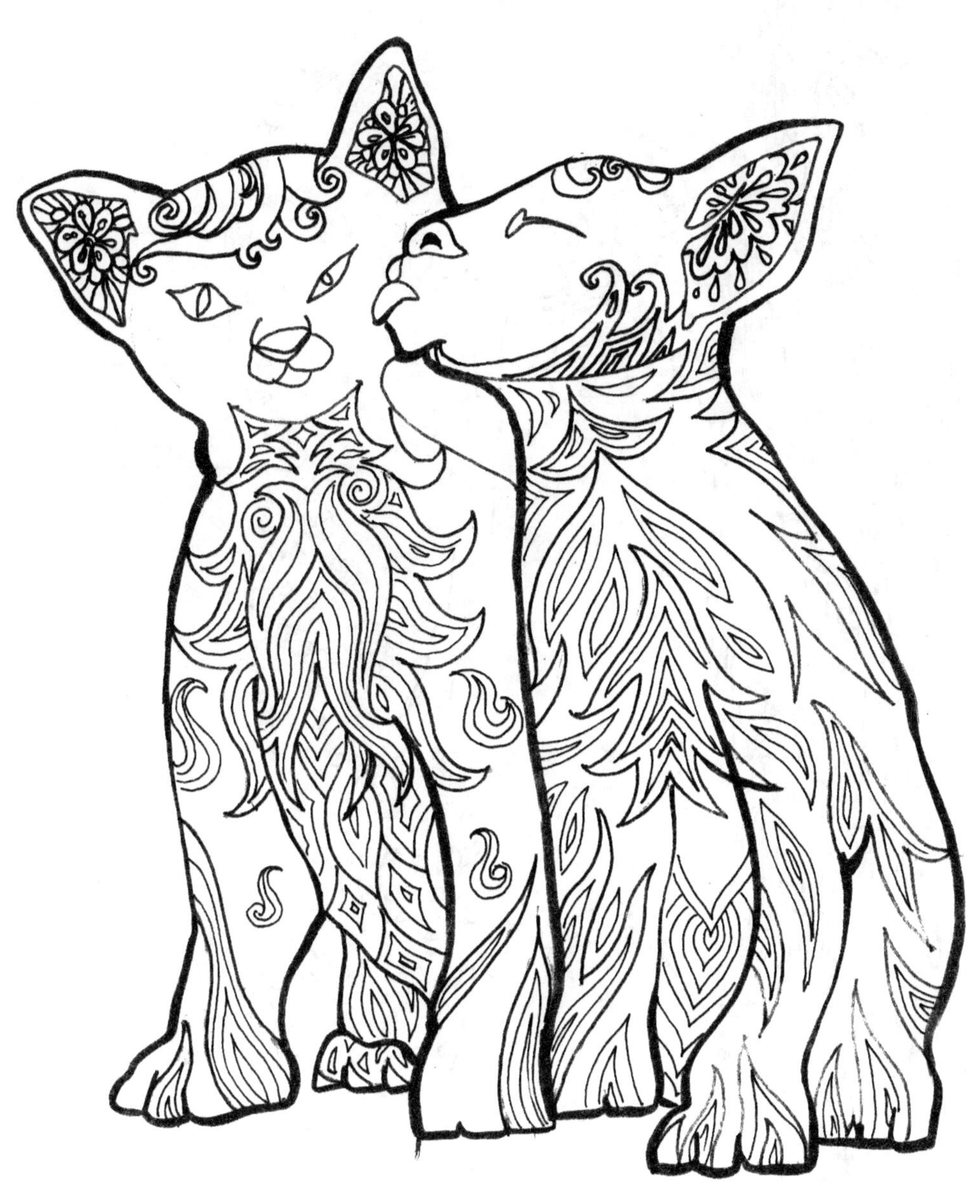

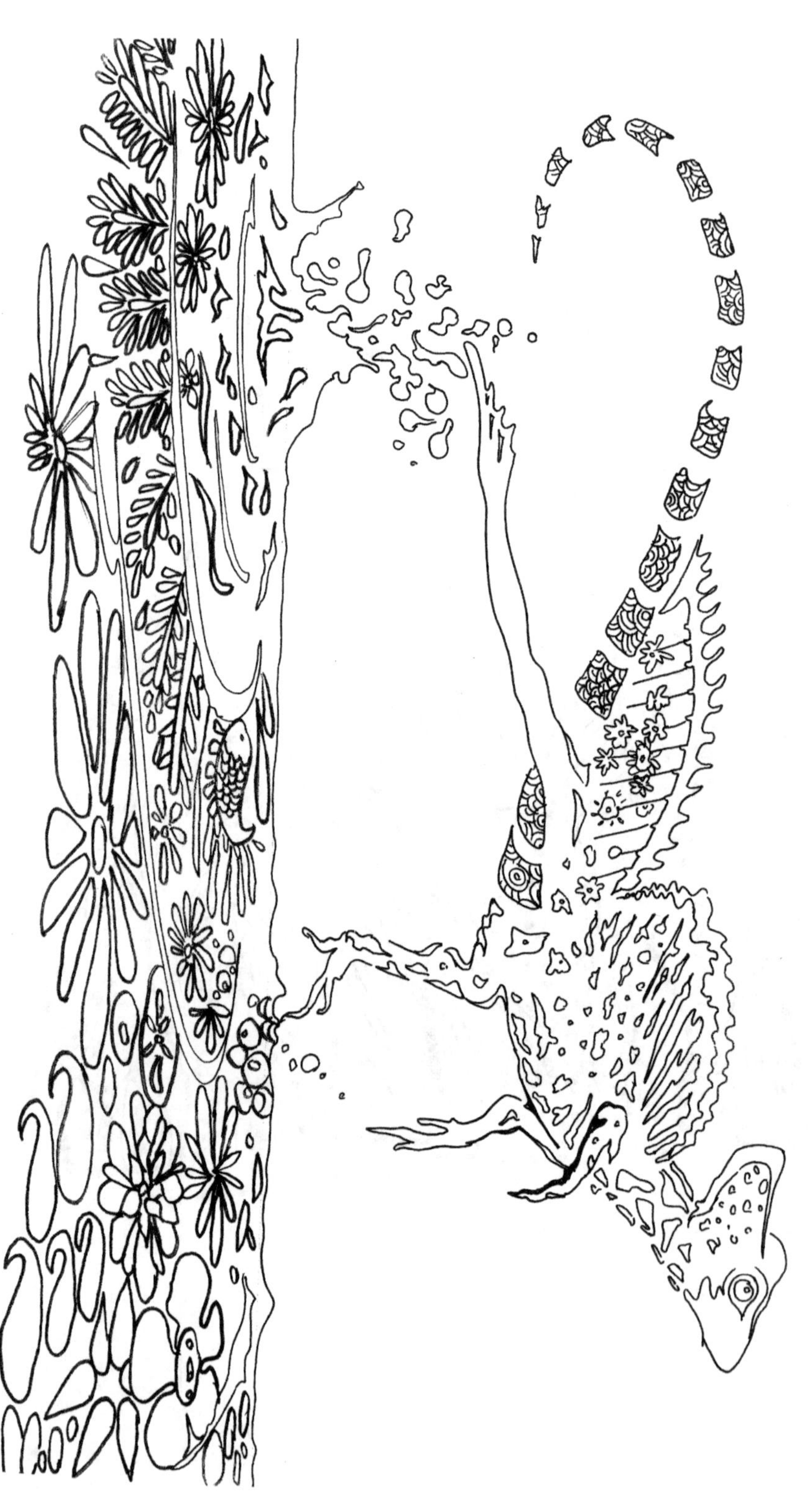

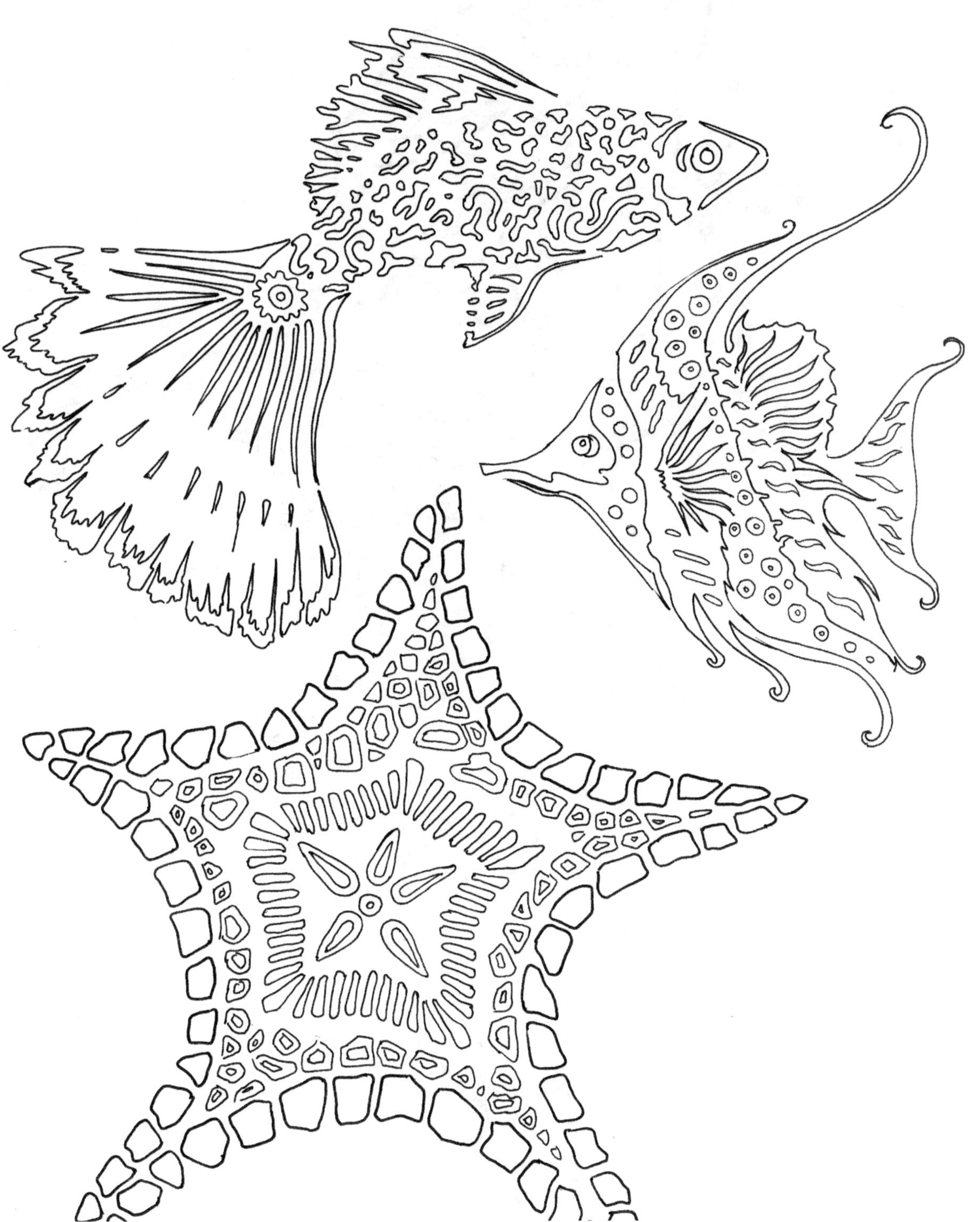

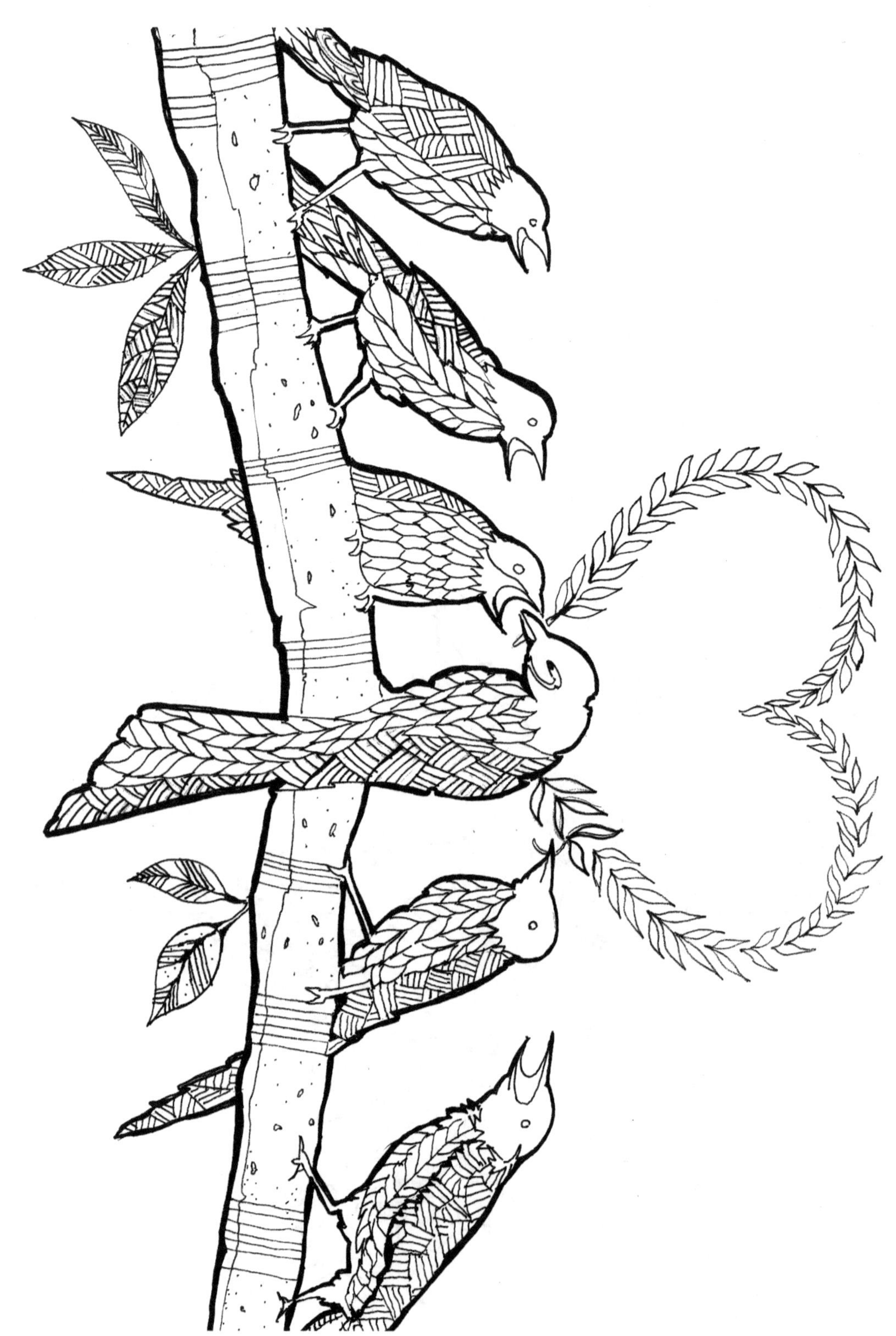

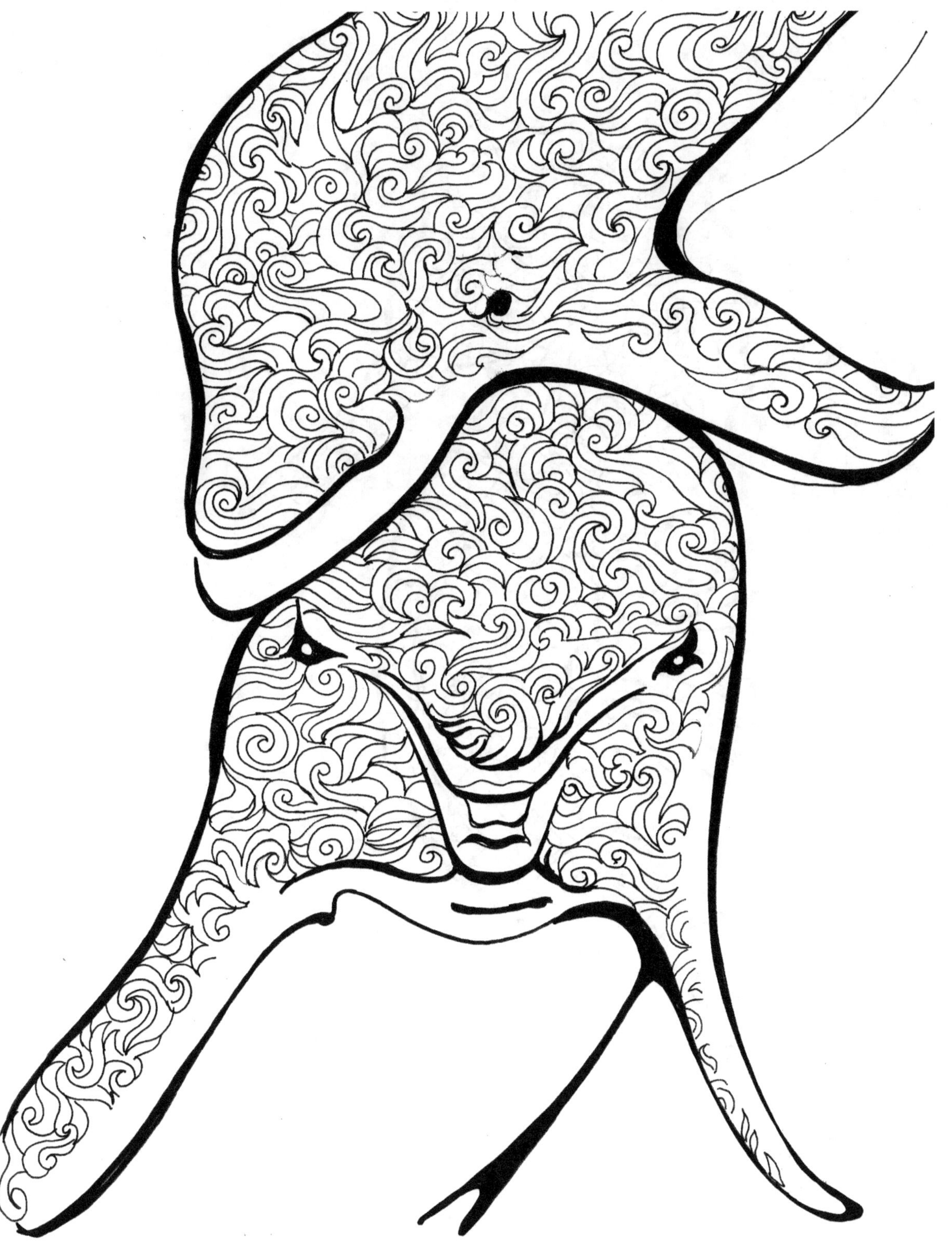

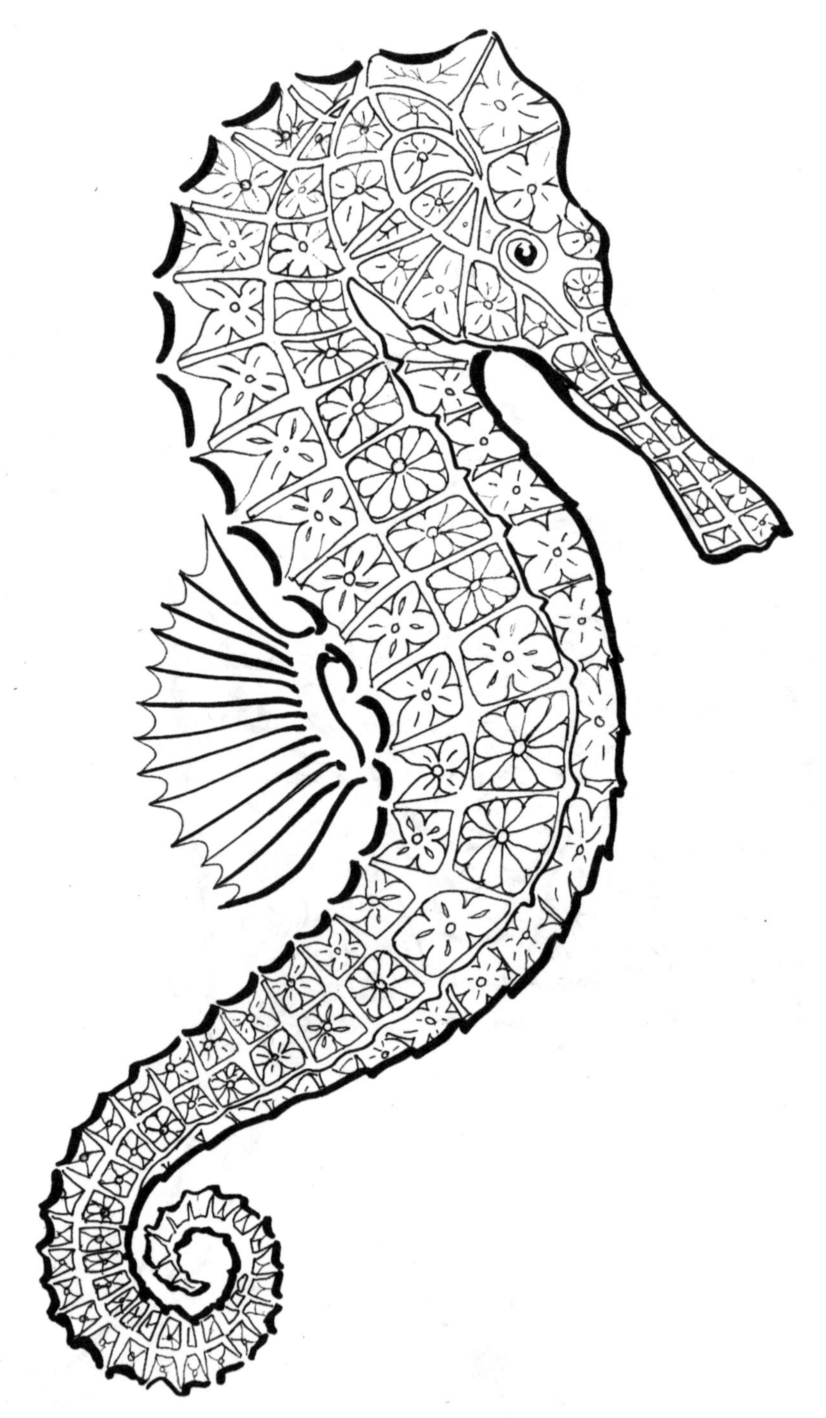

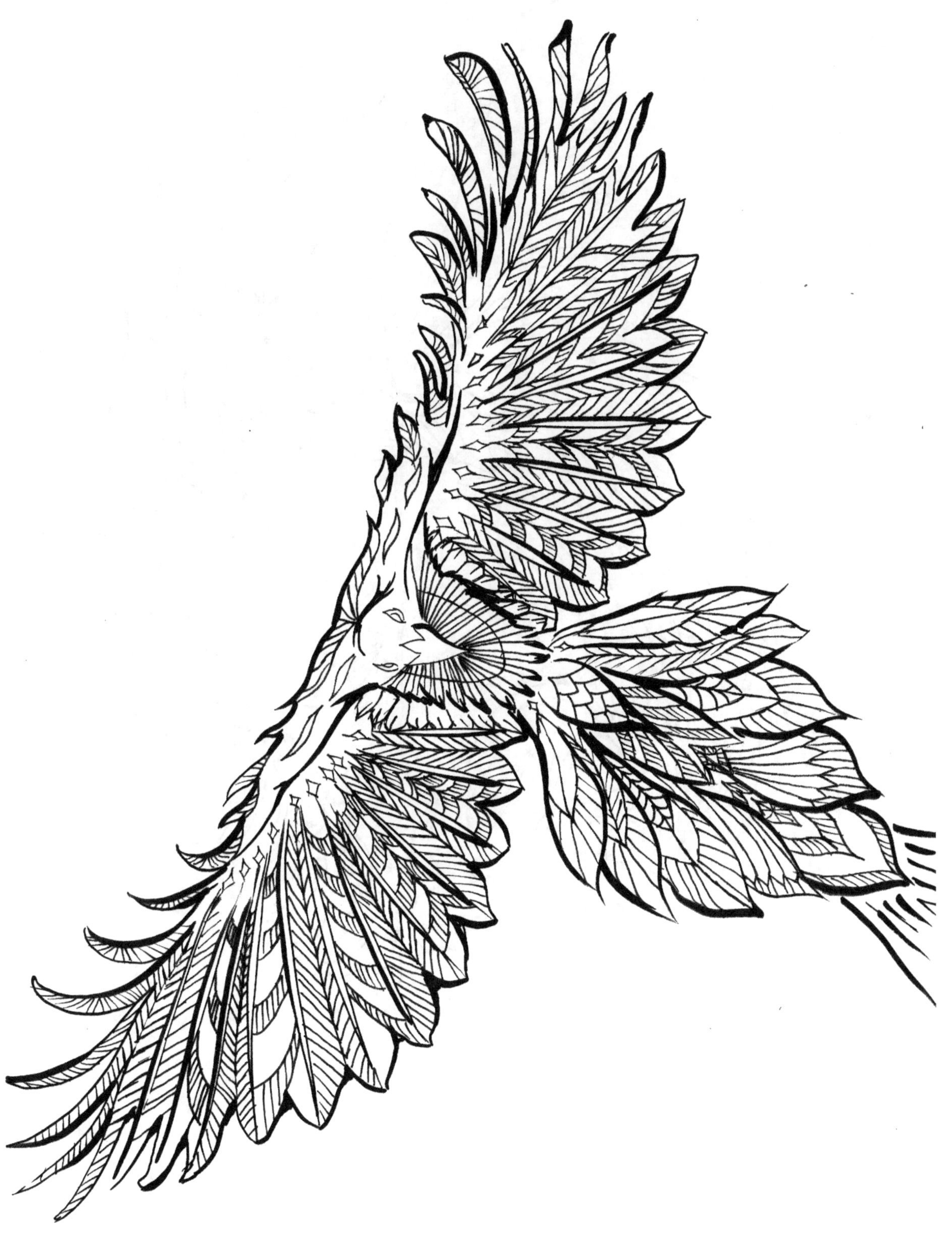

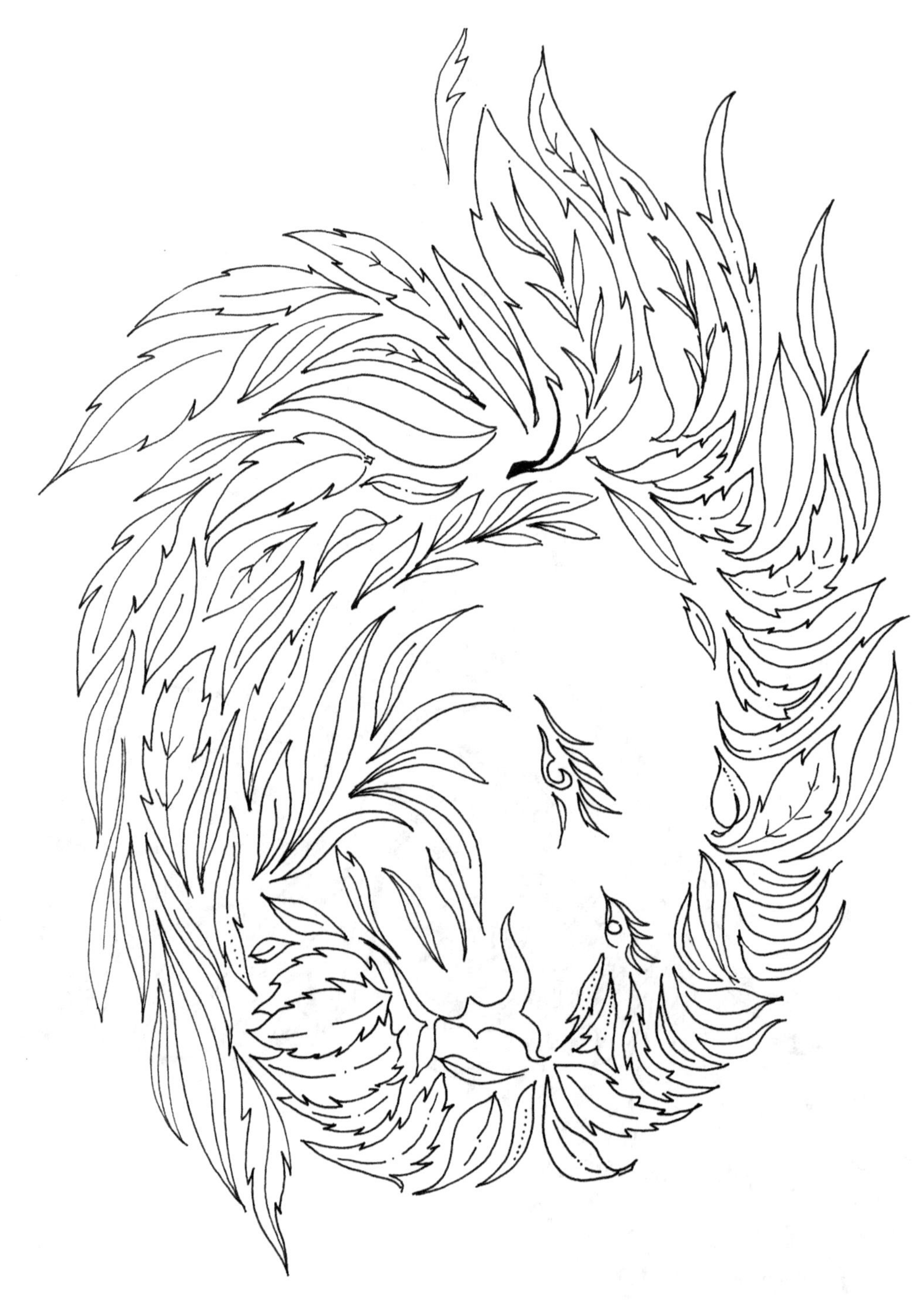

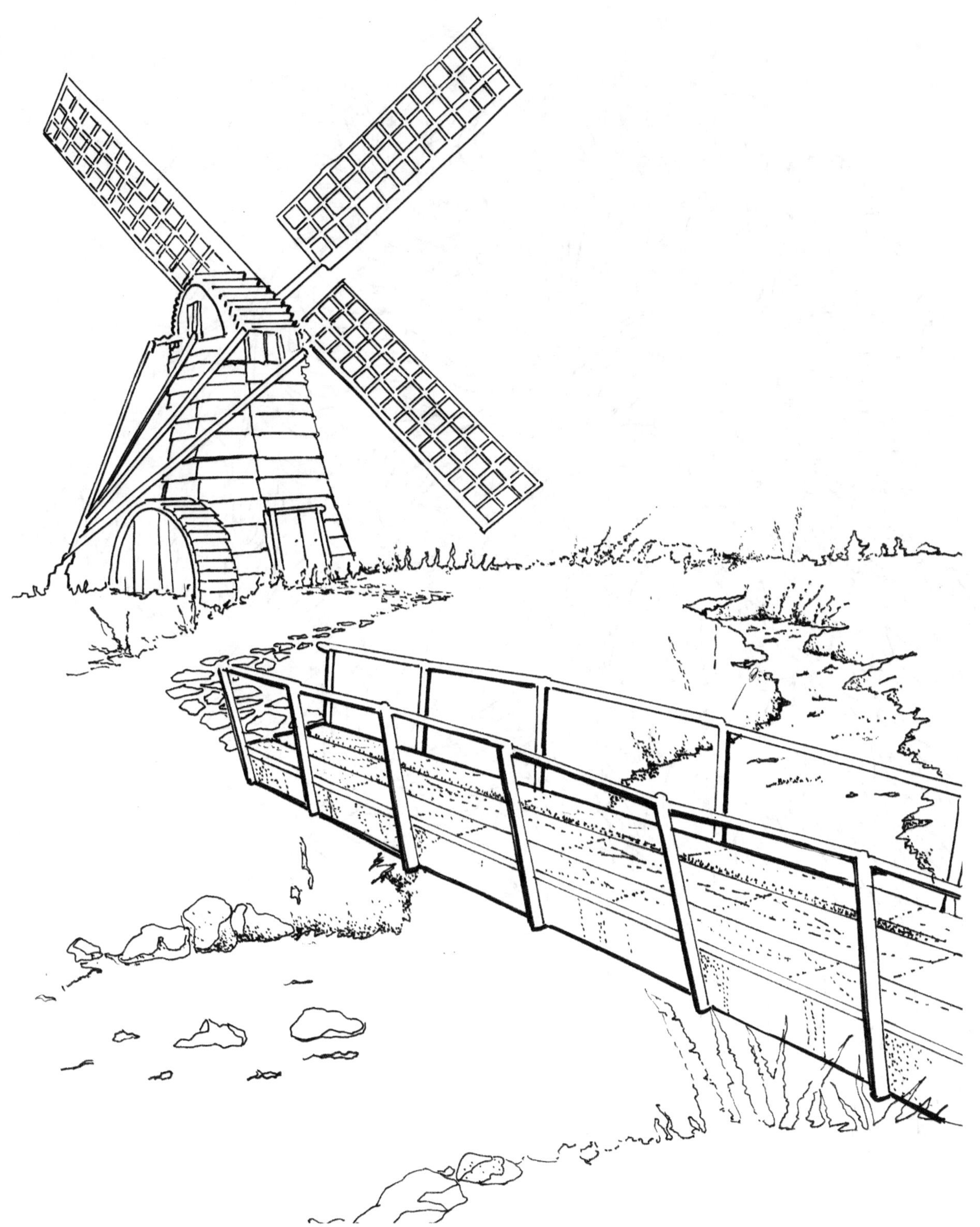

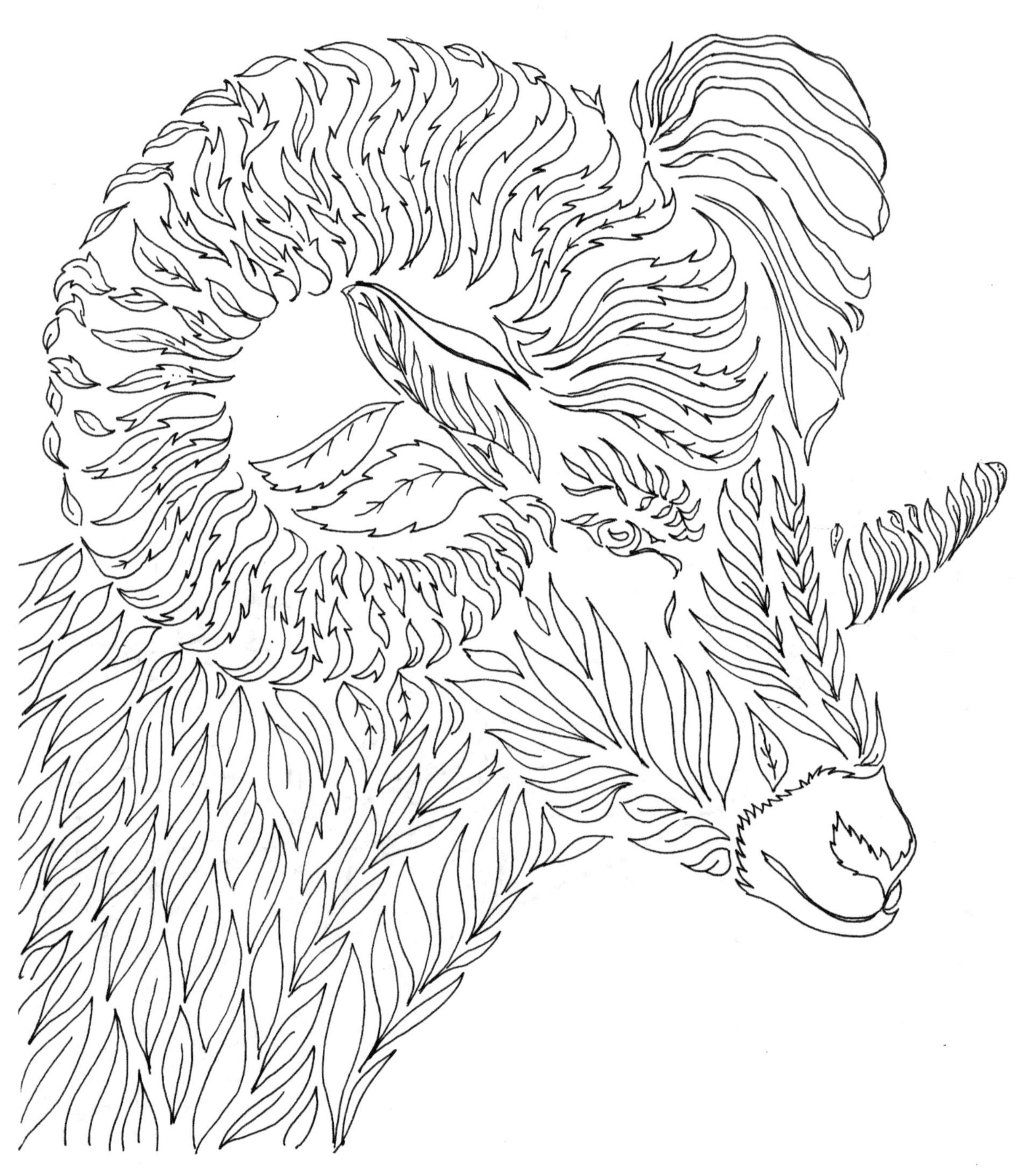

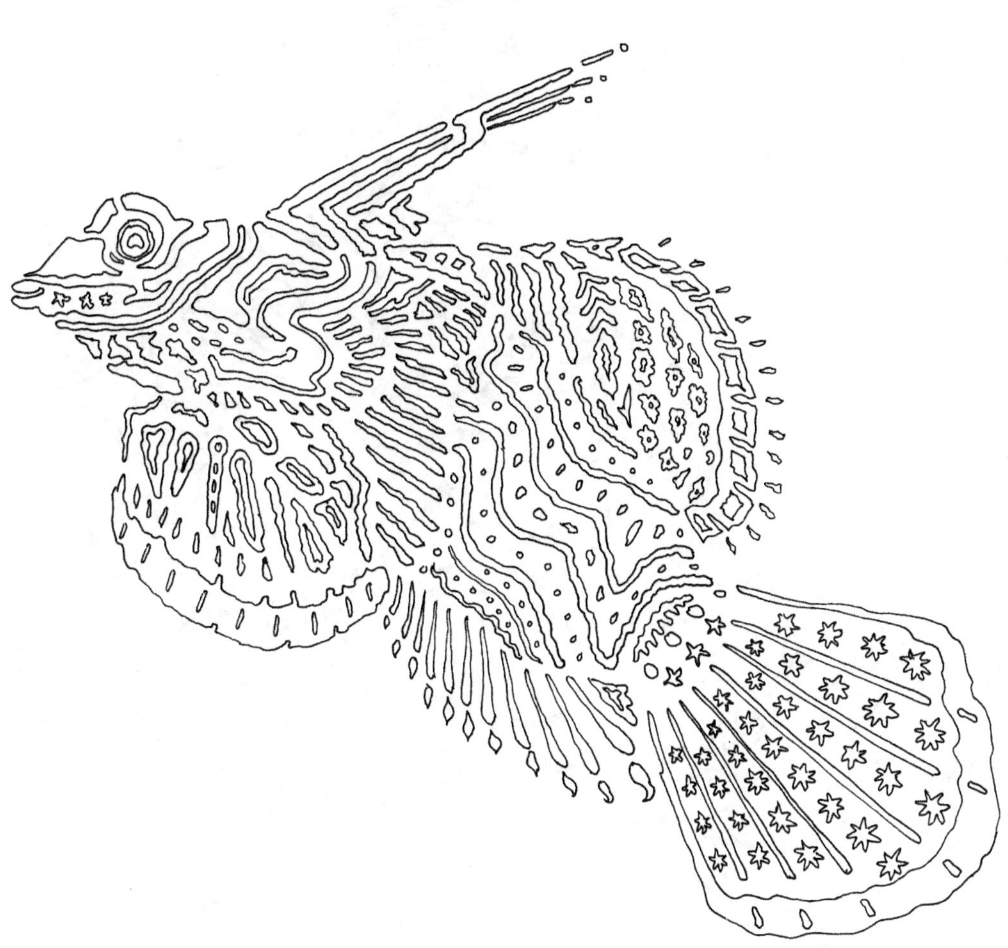

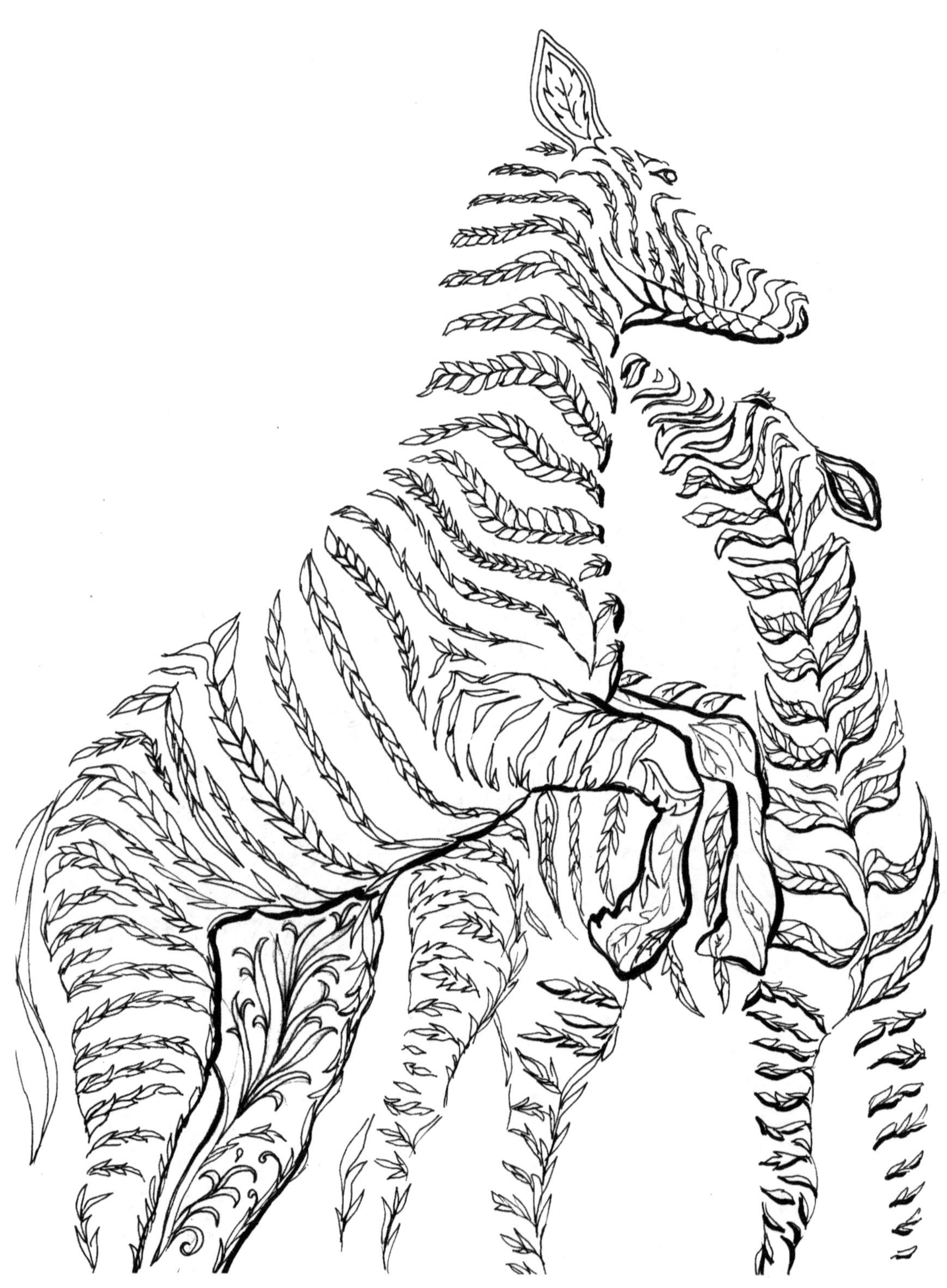

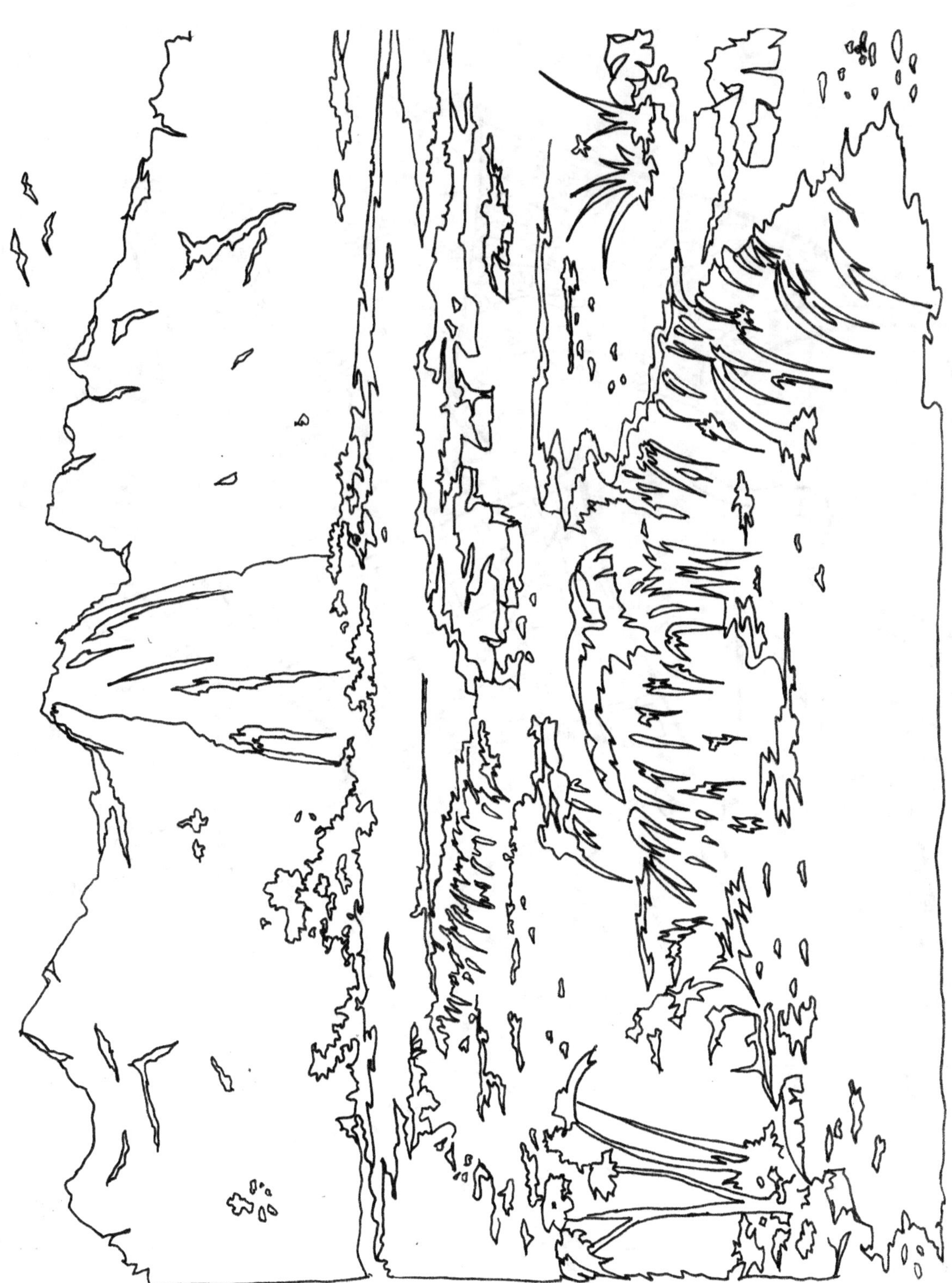

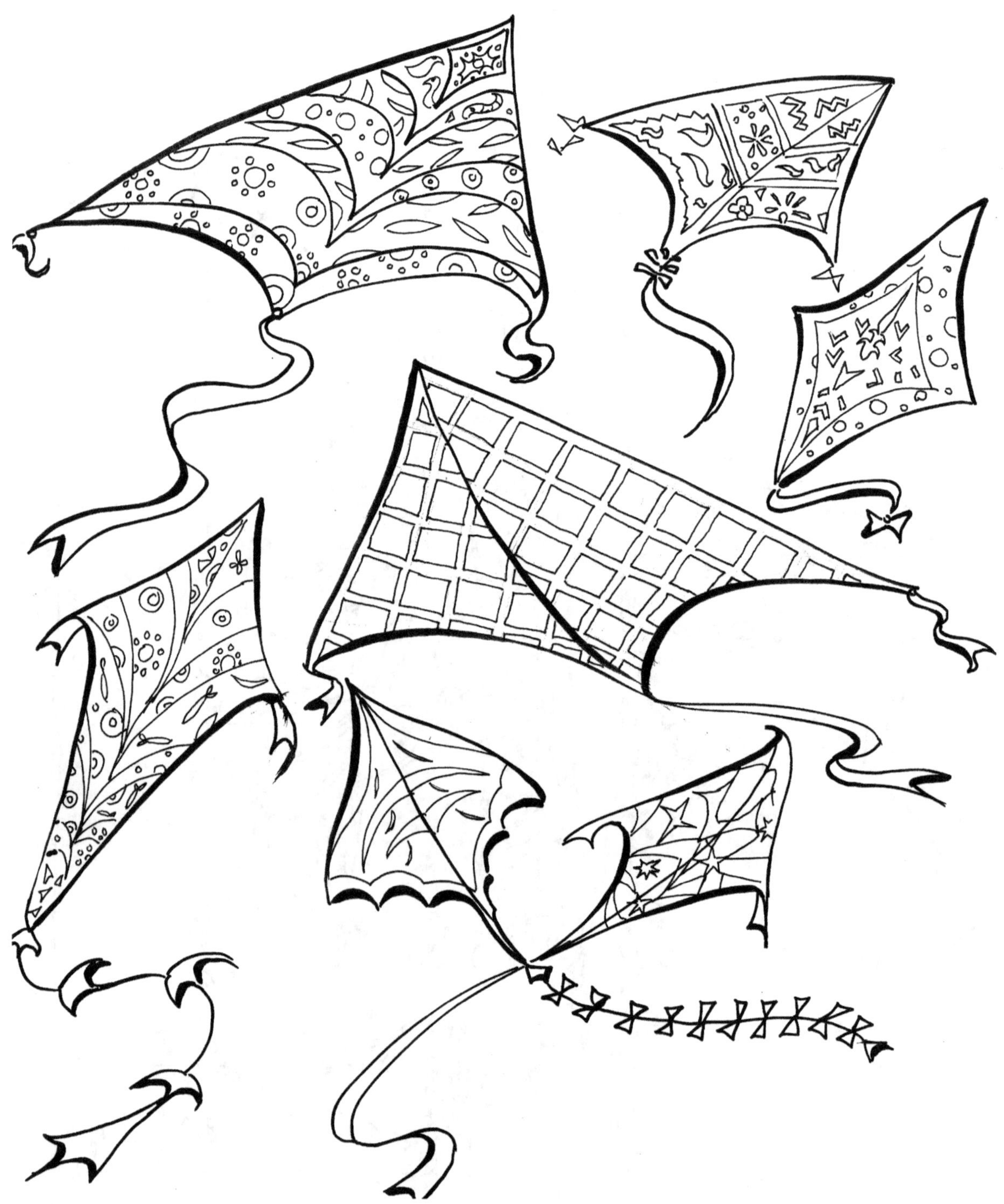

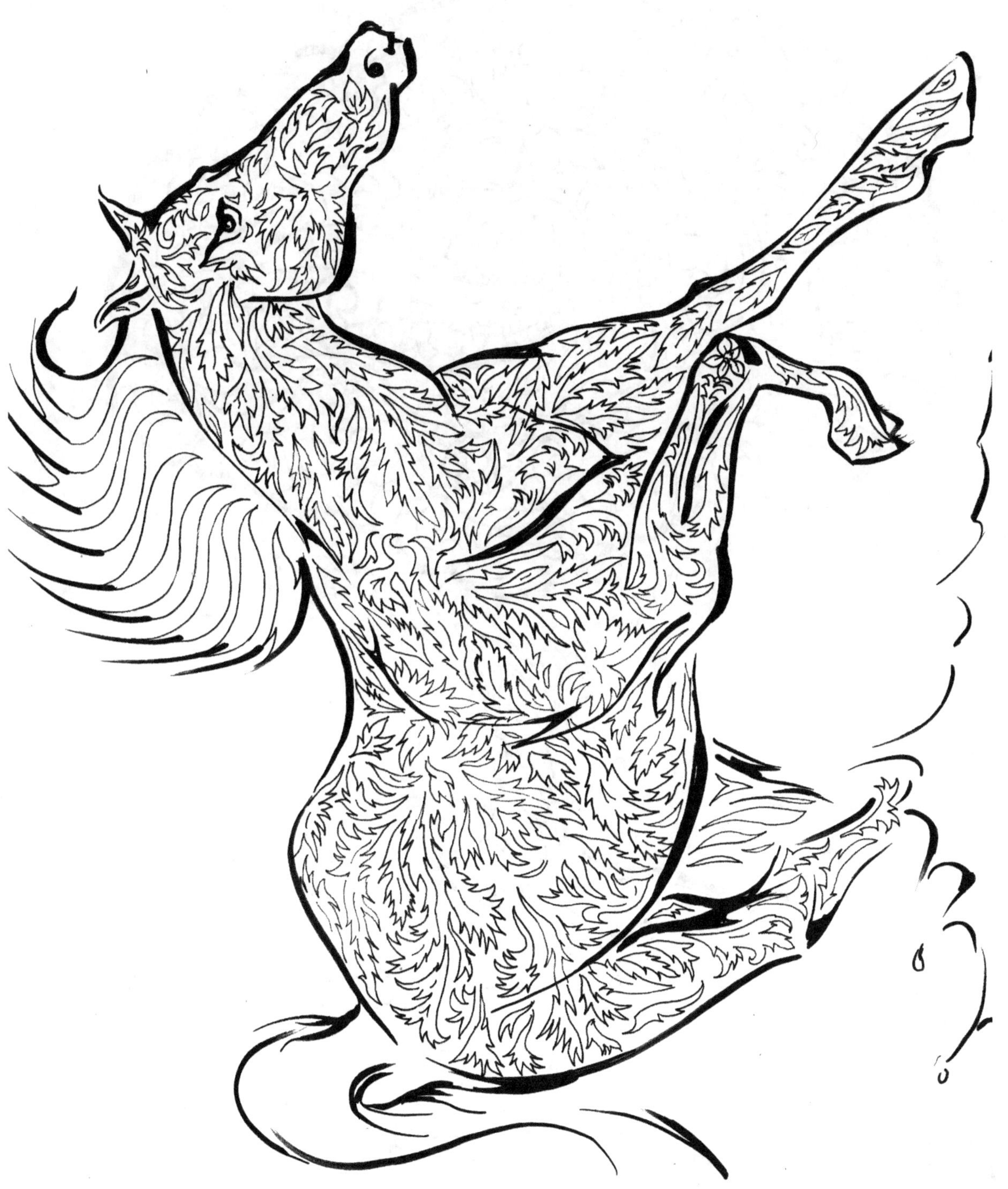

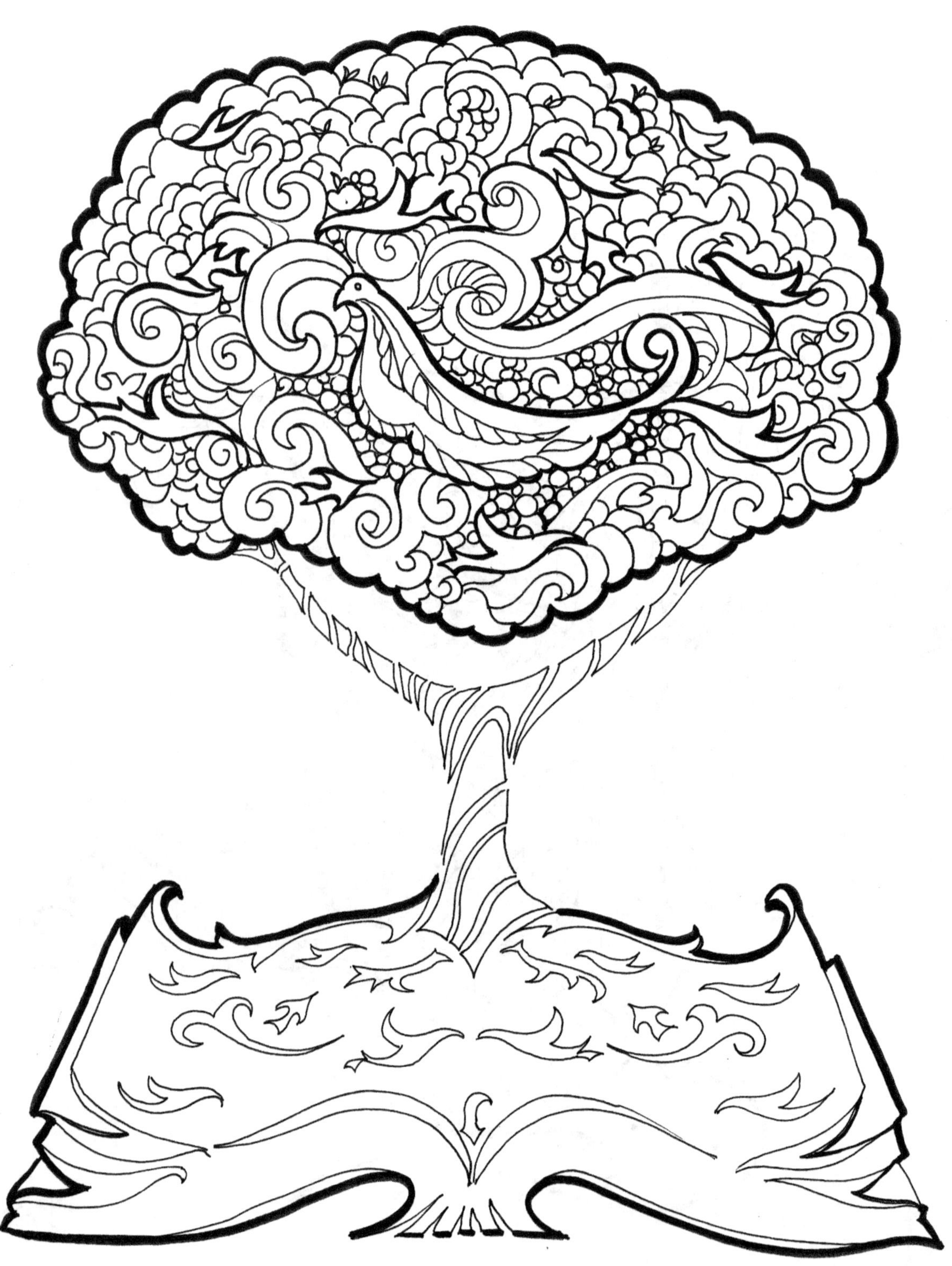

www.ingramcontent.com/pod-product-compliance
Lightning Source LLC
LaVergne TN
LVHW080316110826
845155LV00023B/133